CW00666481

Brenton West

SILVERSMITH'S SECRETS

Brenton West

SILVERSMITH'S SECRETS

Techniques to repair, restore and
transform treasured items

SEARCH PRESS

First published in 2024
Search Press Limited
Wellwood, North Farm Road
Tunbridge Wells, Kent TN2 3DR

Text copyright © Brenton West, 2024
Photographs on pages 1–3, 7, 14–16, 18–24, 30, 74–75, 77,
84(b), 93, 101, 107, 115, 125, 131, 137, 143, 149, 157 and 163,
by Mark Davison; pages 11 and 29, courtesy of Ricochet/
BBC. All others by the author.
Photographs and design © Search Press Ltd, 2024

All rights reserved. No part of this book, text,
photographs or illustrations may be reproduced or
transmitted in any form or by any means by print,
photoprint, microfilm, microfiche, photocopier, video,
internet or in any way known or as yet unknown, or stored
in a retrieval system, without written permission obtained
beforehand from Search Press. Printed in China.

ISBN: 978-1-80092-166-5
ebook ISBN: 978-1-80093-149-7

The Publishers and authors can accept no responsibility
for any consequences arising from the information,
advice or instructions given in this publication.

Suppliers
For details of suppliers, please visit the Search Press
website: www.searchpress.com

Bookmarked
For further ideas and inspiration, and to join our free
online community, visit www.bookmarkedhub.com

You are invited to visit the author's website:
www.brentonwest.co.uk

Publishers' note
All the step-by-step photographs in this book feature
the author, Brenton West, demonstrating silversmithing.
No models have been used.

The projects in this book have been made using metric
measurements, and the imperial equivalents provided
have been calculated following standard conversion
practices. The imperial measurements are rounded to
the nearest ¼in for ease of use. Always use either metric
or imperial measurements, not a combination of both.

DEDICATION

To you, the reader; all aspiring repairers; and to my
two sons, both craftsmen.

ACKNOWLEDGEMENTS

This book has been a labour of love for my craft. It is
extra hard repairing things and photographing it as well!
I would like to thank The London Assay Office
for its help.
I would like to thank Susie, my wife, for reading it
and making suggestions when my grammar and
punctuation may have been a bit astray.
Finally, thanks to my agent David Foster for getting
me this gig.

FSC
www.fsc.org

MIX
Paper | Supporting
responsible forestry
FSC® C016973

CONTENTS

Why write a book on repairing? Because it is important. I am passionate about not wasting anything. My Mum was brought up in the austerity and recession of late 1920s America, and this gave her an incredibly practical and thrifty ethos. She used to say 'I'm a New Englander, and we mend and make things fit for purpose again.' She began delivering yachts across the Atlantic, and then abandoned *terra firma* for a time and lived aboard a yacht for many years. Living on a boat for long stretches of time breeds a certain 'can-do' spirit and thriftiness, which my Mum passed on to me in both conscious and subtler ways. It is for this reason that I know how to sew up torn clothing, darn socks, treat woodworm in furniture, strip paint, sand a floor, varnish a deck(!), paint, dye, cook, marble decorative paper, make candles and so on. It is because of this upbringing that I will always try to fix, rather than replace.

This ethos or attitude of mind has greater traction and relevance for the planet nowadays, more urgently than ever. We have lived in a 'throw-away' culture for so long now and we all know that we need to make changes, both large and small. By fixing and repairing objects, we can gain the satisfaction of making the repair and also help to save the planet: it's win–win.

No matter if an object has great emotional or financial value, if it is broken, it is virtually useless. My goal – and the goal of all silversmiths – is to repair these things to a state where they work properly again or look as fabulous as they possibly can.

Presently, with so few silversmiths left and training establishments closing due to lack of demand and funding, new people need to take up the mantle and give making and repairing a go. I believe and hope that my media exposure has stimulated a whole new group of people. I now want to inspire and encourage you to take that next step and start mending damaged silver, precious objects, and other small metal items.

In this book, I will introduce some regular damaged pieces that you are likely to come across and show you how to fix them. I will discuss the metals, materials and tools you'll need and – whether you're starting out or a seasoned hand – you'll find useful techniques and ideas, many of which are adaptable and transferrable to other projects. With new skills learned or old skills finessed, many supposedly insurmountable challenges can be overcome.

With just a little time and effort, worn, damaged and tired-looking items, like this lamp, can be revitalized – not just made good, but brought to a level of finish of which you can be rightly proud, as shown opposite.

WHERE DID IT ALL START?

I was very inquisitive, always getting my fingers stuck in somewhere or breaking things to test how strong they were. I would pull up floorboards to see where wires and pipes went, I would open the dishwasher to see what went on inside when it was working. My entertainment was learning how things worked and making things. This incessant curiosity sometimes didn't go down so well with my parents!

Later, when I became more dexterous, I would take things apart to see how they functioned. Sometimes they would reassemble correctly, often not. But this is how I learned. I tried to stick a toy car back together with melted wax – that just didn't work. I tried various glues: all the wrong ones! I finally managed to stick it back together with my mum's sealing wax and a lighter. In doing this, I burned my fingers, but I had triumphed. I learned from experiences like these, through trial and error, until I struck upon success.

At primary school, art and craft lessons seemed to be all about gluing a few collages and making some papier-mâché three-dimensional figures. This did not quench my thirst for creating and making things. Plastic and balsa aeroplane kits became one of my favourite constructive pastimes. After school I watched television shows like *Blue Peter* and *How?*; practical programmes that showed projects for children to make and do. I used to make many of the 'here is one I prepared earlier' activities. I remember emptying my Mum's washing-up liquid bottle into a jar, so I could use the container to make the character Dougal from *The Magic Roundabout*.

I recall going to a bicycle shop in Kentish Town where the mechanic showed me how to get the tyre off and fix a puncture. I was chuffed to bits – it was amazing being able to do these things myself.

Later, I would go to the council tip in Camden Town and scrounge old television sets and radios that had been thrown away. I would take them home using my Mum's two-wheeled shopping basket tied to the back of the bike as a makeshift trailer.

In my bedroom-cum-workshop I found that by wiggling the valves I could often get them to work again – though I confess, I did get the odd shock: a lesson all of its own!

Early start

When my mother recently passed away and I cleared her belongings, I found jewellery that I had made for her as a child – beads on strings and a ring made from a metal coke bottle top, rubber band and glitter!

I learned how to turn my hand to many practical jobs, including car mechanics.

If I couldn't fix these old sets, I would take the speaker out (as they were useful for home-fangled hi-fi) take the electrics out and use the wood from the cases to make other small projects, such as jewellery boxes or speaker cabinets.

On a trip to Scotland with my mum when I was about ten, we stayed in a friend's house on a mountain side. I found a roll of soft solder wire and a soldering iron in the under-stairs cupboard. I started making ridiculous rings and bracelets, I plaited wire, made earrings from paper clips and copper wire, I soldered metal using the soldering iron. This was the first time that I recall joining two bits of metal together correctly. I found by hammering the metal, while it was supported on something hard (a vice), I could make decorative 'flats' on its surface.

In my very early teens, I would be allowed to turn my dad's car round on his driveway in exchange for vacuuming the car's carpets. One time, in my eagerness to have a drive, I ran over the aluminium end of the flexible hose, almost flattening it. In fear of getting into terrible trouble I went into the garage and found a metal tapered pole used for banging into the ground to break up hardcore and concrete. I hit this pole into the end of the tube to make it sort-of round, then tapped around the outside with a block of wood. I managed to make the hose round again and therefore machine serviceable. No-one even noticed!

Early steps – base metal articles that I made at school.

MY PATH TO SILVERSMITHING

In the early 1970s, there was political unrest in the UK which caused an energy crisis. One of the impacts of this was that we had many power cuts. It was known as The Three Day Week. I saw an opportunity. I went to the local churches and asked if I could have their old candle stumps. After a while, I had a sack full of them. I melted them down and filtered the burned wicks from the residue. Then, with new wicks and colouring, and using moulds from the candle-making suppliers on Parkway, Camden Town, I recycled the wax into quite passable candles. I went around my neighbourhood selling them. I always sold out. I don't think people felt sorry for me – they had a need, they really liked the candle designs and I was there to help them. I found being creative was very rewarding on several levels. People actually wanted something that I had made, which pleased me no end – that they were willing to pay for it was a bonus.

I had an amazing metalwork teacher at secondary school. Frank was a young master and a great character, delighting in our company. He inspired us all. We made objects from copper, brass and gilding metal. In metalwork I learned to fabricate base-metal decorative pieces. I also learned to make a mould and then cast molten metal. I was taught how to use a lathe, I even made iron fire-side accessories on a blacksmith's forge. We were taught to measure, draw and design. I was in my element. The subjects that I was encouraged to learn to get me into university were sorely neglected. My desire to live my day mostly in the metalwork room meant that I failed my A-level exams. But to me that didn't matter. I had other ideas about how I was going to make a living. It certainly was not going to be about going to university to study law or accountancy. It had to be art or craft; I had to be using my hands. I had to be a 'maker'.

pewter. Small items from £6,
larger from £10. No travel.
Oxfordshire: Brenton West, 5
Park Lane, East Lockinge,
Wantage. (East Hendred 754).
Works mainly in silver, some
gold. Jewelry repairs (not
claw settings), makes tops
for salt cellars, ink stands.
Three Goldsmiths awards for
chasing and silversmithing.
Area — anywhere in Oxon.

Newspaper article to drum up business, from around 1981.

Here's me hard at work in my first workshop, on a sheep farm in Oxfordshire.

Armed with my portfolio of beakers, a goblet, a candle-snuffer and a box (yes, my mum kept those too!), I managed to gain a place at the highly acclaimed Medway College of Design, one of the UK's top silversmithing colleges. There I was taught by very skilled craftsmen, who were the UK's top silversmiths and jewellers at the time. Names such as Bob May, Norman Bassant, Ian Calvert, Dave May and Brian May were my tutors and taught me my trade. I didn't know that at the time, or fully appreciate it. But when I am working on something today, I often think back to when I was at college learning these skills. It was an extremely rich and beneficial time for me that I have taken with me all the way.

Those three years gave me the ability and confidence to tackle just about any repair. I had gained three Goldsmiths awards, a Johnson Matthey Metals design award, eight City & Guilds certificates and a Diploma in Silversmithing and Allied Crafts.

TURNING PROFESSIONAL

Having completed three years of art college, at the tender age of twenty, I moved to Oxfordshire to set up my own silversmithing business. Even though the first and foremost aim of my silver business was to create beautiful objects that could be sold, inevitably repairs often turned out to be the 'bread and butter' of a silversmithing workshop. The beginning was hard. I earned very little money and had to augment my coffers with what you might call a 'proper' job, so during the evenings and weekends, I taught silversmithing part-time at a reputable Oxford college.

My skills were learned at school and college, then have expanded and developed throughout my lifetime. Today not only can I knock a dent out of a precious silver teapot, but I can also rebuild classic cars. I can build and renovate houses and make a table or a wooden kitchen from scratch.

My thirst for creativity and boundless (one could say almost hyperactive) need to be doing something makes me continue to want to learn new skills and improve the ones that I already possess. My journey to becoming the silver and metals' expert and a regular on the much-loved, award winning BBC One programme *The Repair Shop* has been through some twists and turns. By broadcasting the repairs, I hope that I am inspiring a new generation of artisan craftspeople and fixers, young and old.

By far and away the biggest reward for what I do is that I glean so much pleasure from hearing positive messages from happy and satisfied clients. I often hear, 'We were told it could never be fixed'. Smiling faces are a most gratifying and extra bonus.

I will go on making and fixing as long as I possibly can.

At my bench in the studio barn of The Repair Shop.

SILVERSMITHING

Silver has been used by craftspeople since ancient times. Mined and used mainly for coins – the ancient Greeks used silver coins as early as 350BC – it was also used to make jewellery, vessels, cutlery and other decorative metal items, a practice now known as silversmithing.

In the modern era, wealthy families would have handmade silver pieces in their homes as a show of their affluence. During the industrial revolution, new manufacturing techniques such as stamping, spinning and casting allowed more affordable items to be created than pieces made by hand by individual craftspeople. New techniques and approaches to boost profit were employed during this period. Cutlery sets were stamped out, making them affordable to far more people than in the past. Picture frames were manufactured with incredibly thin metal, and then filled with a heavy filler such as pitch. This lent support to the frail, nearly paper-thin silver, and gave the objects strength and a 'weighty', valuable feel.

Silver that is made today tends to be more bespoke than the glory days of the Industrial Revolution. Silver production mainly consists of many craftspeople practising their art and making individual items. There are still commercial manufacturers but these are few and far between.

Before

WHAT IS A SILVERSMITH?

At root, silversmithing is the specialist craft of making or repairing anything from silver. Unlike goldsmiths, who tend to specialize in jewellery due to the great expense of gold, a silversmith needs to be versatile, and will be able to turn their hand to make (or repair) a wide range of objects from most metals. As a silversmith, for example, I have worked on the likes of classic cars made from aluminium to the other extreme – a priceless 23.5 carat gold Nobel prize medal.

Silversmithing continues to evolve, melding old skills with new ideas. I was taught in the traditions of silversmithing by very skilled tutors, and I also enjoy seeing the latest ideas and techniques that new silversmiths come up with – the imagination and skills of the current top silversmiths are something to behold.

The craft of silversmithing has evolved over the years and it is fairly – though not always – easy to guess in which period a piece was made by the design vogue or trend it demonstrates. When I was trained, for example, texturing with a hammer, engraver or rotary burr was all the rage, as was adding gilding.

METALSMITHS

While craft metalsmiths tend to specialize in a particular metal, each will have the tools in their armoury and the skillset to work in different metals – a coppersmith can work in silver, a silversmith can work in gold and so forth.

A blacksmith's work differs slightly again from these specialisms. Concerned with forming iron and steel, the majority of their shaping is done when the metal is red hot. I learned blacksmithing at school and found it very rewarding.

The finished repair

HOW DO I BECOME A SILVERSMITH?

Silversmiths training can take different routes. Art colleges offer (usually) a three-year degree course in silversmithing. Another avenue into the trade could be to complete a pre-apprentice course. By doing this you would become equipped (hopefully) to gain an apprenticeship with an established silversmith.

I took the art college route. When a silversmithing exam took place at college, half a dozen people would be hitting metal for all that they were worth, all day. The din was immense. At the college our department's members had the nickname 'tinbashers' – can't imagine why!

After three years of studying, making and learning, diploma under my arm, I arrived in the big world of real life. I was ill-equipped to turn these skills into making a living. I was proficient in making lovely pieces but had no experience in the nuts and bolts of running a business. I also had no idea and experience in the art of repairing objects; I was just a maker.

Those skills – namely, being able to identify an issue or damage and deal with it while causing the least disruption to the original piece – come with time. Problem solving and patience are the key to success.

It is vital for a person who makes a living practising an art to be diverse in what they can do. A qualified silversmith may have aspirations of creating commissions for clients, but to be able to repair pieces when the phone isn't ringing for those commissions can be a very handy revenue stream.

There are so few people repairing that there is a goldmine (excuse the pun) in the market for anyone who desires to use their skills in this manner. I so often hear 'It has been broken for ages, I just couldn't find anyone who could repair it'.

I have a lust for creativity and repairing a seemingly irreparable object fulfils that desire. I always photograph a piece before I fix it. Sometimes it is staggering to see the difference.

WHAT DOES THIS BOOK DO?

You do not need to be a silversmith to be able to use this book. There are many techniques and tricks that will have a broad appeal to anyone who wants to fix anything. I believe that fixing and repairing are so important. By knowing how various metals behave, I hope that this book will help your journey into becoming a better craftsperson. I have used my many years of working in the trade to demonstrate some typical examples of repairs that one can come across. I hope that the repairs that are shown practically will stimulate many others to have a go when they are ready.

My methods show the way in which I tackle a repair. In these projects later in the book you can see the procedures that worked well for me, but bear in mind there may be other ways around solving the repair that work equally as well. In the interests of brevity, I show only one.

The 'fixes' in this book were all repaired by me in my home-built barn. I make no excuses for the close-ups of dirty fingernails!

A DAY IN THE LIFE OF A SILVERSMITH

A silversmith often works alone, but has contact with other craftspeople to complement their craft. I have engravers, platers, jewellers and fabricators in my phone book and often give my pieces to them for their avenue of skill or expertise to enhance my creation or repair.

I start my day by checking my email, doing quotes and estimates for the stream of enquiries.

When a piece arrives at my workshop, it is photographed. I then put the date of its arrival in a ledger. It then has its place in the queue. It is tempting to fix the easy object or the fun repair. However, for me it is important to stick to my rule of working through projects in their order on the list. Each piece moves up as jobs ahead are returned.

I then write and print invoices, pack up what I have fixed previously and post it back to the owners. I always use guaranteed and insured postage.

Once the admin is complete, I go to my workshop and plan what I am doing for the day. Sometimes I may fix two or three items in a day, sometimes I might work for several weeks on a single commission.

If things are not going well, it is important to step back. Stop what you are doing and move on to something else. Giving yourself thinking space for a tricky job often results in you finding a solution. Rarely, have I thought that 'this is impossible' or 'I cannot do this'. With persistence and a good plan, most things can be overcome. There is nothing wrong with seeking advice from others.

Metal guide

When attempting a repair on an item, it's important to know which metals you're working with. Sometimes this seems obvious, but looks can be deceiving. This chapter gives you an overview of the most common metals you will find yourself working with, and how you can identify them. Once identified, you'll be better equipped to plan which tools and techniques you'll need, and know its particular qualities, such as its melting point.

IDENTIFYING METALS

To repair an object, you need to know for sure what it's made from – see my experience with a 'silver' teapot on page 54 to see why! The following tips are starting points for assessing what metal an object is made from.

Properties If you have a similar object of a known metal, comparing qualities like weight, softness or magnetism can give you a lead on identification.

Scratch test If you own the object, try scratching it somewhere unobtrusive. If the surface is plated, this will remove the top silver layer, revealing the base metal. This could be copper, brass, or nickel, which you can assess by colour. If it is white metal, it will feel soft, like lead.

Appearance Metals vary widely in appearance. The following pages show close-ups of various metals; comparing the object with each and seeing which is closest in appearance will give you a starting point.

Hallmark The presence of a hallmark (see pages 24–29) is a surefire sign the object is either silver, gold, platinum or palladium – but beware false marks, as shown below.

TESTING SILVER

This fork has some markings that are likely intended to look like hallmarks, but on closer inspection are meaningless, throwing the material into doubt. Fortunately, there are a couple of simple ways to check the credentials of a supposedly silver item.

If, after trying the scratch test (see above), you are still not sure, a silver test kit can be used. If you put a drop of silver testing solution on a genuine piece of silver, the solution will turn red. If the object is plated, it will turn green.

Scraping to test
Use a sharp blade to scrape a little area of an item. Choose somewhere discreet at the back, the bottom, or otherwise out of sight.

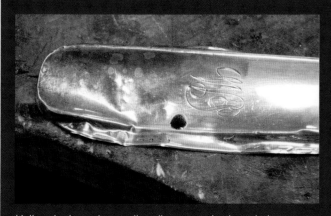

Hallmarked genuine sterling silver control – the solution turns red.

On this silver-plated fork, the scraped test area turns green.

SILVER

Silver is a highly shiny, white element. It is ductile and malleable – properties that make it very suitable for making vessels, cutlery, coins and jewellery. Silver is also antibacterial and antiseptic, making it an appropriate metal for food vessels and eating utensils.

Silver items should bear a correct hallmark somewhere on them – see pages 24–29 for more on hallmarks. This will give you certainty over the particular quality of silver used.

Fine In its pure form silver is called 'fine'. This means that the metal is 999 parts per 1000 pure silver. This is too soft to be durable for jewellery or items that are used regularly and therefore subject to wear and tear. However, the malleability of fine silver makes it very appropriate for chasing and repousse, which are methods of silver decoration that use punches to create raised embellishments. Fine silver has a melting point of 961°C (1762°F).

Sterling Sterling silver is by far the most common form of silver and is widely used in the craft trade. Its quality, defined by the UK Assay Office, is 925 parts silver per 1000 with the balance mainly comprising copper. A 925 mark is often seen on smaller items to indicate their quality. Sterling silver melts at 890°C (1634°F). It can be bought as sheet, rod, bar, tube, wire or casting granules, as well as an array of 'findings' from silversmithing bullion suppliers. It is not uncommon to require silver sheet for patching a hole or a delicate silver tube for repairing worn or broken hinges.

Britannia Britannia silver has melting point of 940°C (1724°F). Its composition is 958 parts silver per 1000, with the balance mainly copper. The standard was introduced by Act of Parliament to replace sterling silver, but complaints were made by silversmiths that it was too soft and sterling was reintroduced in 1720, although the Britannia standard remains to this day. It is important not to confuse Britannia standard silver with Britannia metal. The latter does not contain any silver.

800 Another standard that is hallmarked but rarely used. As the name suggests, it is made up of 800 parts silver to 200 parts other metals.

Silver is my favourite metal. It is fantastic to work with and I find the finish alluring. This silver bowl is a 'freeform' chased bowl approximately 300mm (11¾in) in diameter. It feels as if the silver flows, not unlike a liquid.

SILVERSMITH'S SECRET: FIRESTAIN

Sterling and Britannia silver both suffer from an affliction called firestain. This is an unsightly reddish-purple stain that appears on silver after it is heated. It is a reaction between the oxygen in the air and the copper in the alloy.

Firestain needs to be removed by sanding or filing before polishing, or you can silver-plate over the top of it.

Preventive measures can be taken to avoid it happening in the first place, too. Protective barriers (usually flux-based) can be painted onto the surface of the silver before it is heated. They are not perfect and you will always get a bit of firestain, but they help to keep the removal work of firestain to a minimum. I use Argotect, a white powder that is mixed with methylated spirit. This evaporates quickly or burns off when you start heating the item.

GOLD

Gold is a soft, heavy, yellow element. Commonly used for fine jewellery like my pictured wristwatch, it is available in well-known standards: 9ct, 14ct, 18ct, 22ct and 24ct. (9ct contains 375 parts gold per 1000; 18ct 750/1000 and so on.) It can be manipulated and soldered in a similar way to silver, with melting temperature of 1064°C (1947°F).

Gold maintains its polish and rarely tarnishes. Like silver, gold items should bear a hallmark.

COPPER

Copper is an element. Copper is soft, red coloured, and very malleable. It is often used as a cheaper metal for manufacture, as it can be plated to look like silver.

Working in copper is slightly easier than silver as it is softer; however, it is a very 'dirty' metal to work with – when copper is heated to anneal, it produces copious amounts of black-brown oxide that need to be removed. I find the smell of the copper oxide unpleasant.

Copper is relatively cheap and so great for the beginner silversmith to practise on. This delightful watering can, which can be seen in full on page 70, is an example of the coppersmith's art.

BRASS

Brass is an alloy made from copper and zinc. The relatively low melting point of brass – around 900–940°C (1652–1724°F) depending on the ratio of its components – makes it a relatively easy material to cast.

Altering the ratio of copper and zinc, or by combining it with tin, lead, iron, aluminium, manganese, silicon or arsenic, will change the properties or malleability of the finished brass. Unfortunately this makes it hard to know exactly what alloy is present and therefore how to work with it.

BRONZE

Bronze is an alloy of copper and tin, sometimes with other elements added to the mix, such as phosphorus or aluminium.

It is generally used for casting: the molten bronze is poured into moulds to make items such as sculptures. Large and complicated bronzes are often cast in several pieces and joined together. It is useful to know this when repairing a broken bronze piece.

NICKEL

Nickel is an element which is silvery with a touch of gold to its tint. It is ductile, polishes well and is fairly resistant to tarnishing.

It was once used for coins and cutlery (later to be silver-plated) but its high cost has now seen it fall out of favour for use in these products. It is mainly now used to electro-plate other metals, which stops them corroding. Its melting temperature is 1455°C (2651°F).

EPNS stands for 'electro-plated nickel silver', and is used to refer to an item made from nickel and subsequently silver-plated.

GILDING METAL

An alloy made up of 95% copper and 5% zinc, gilding metal is quite dark gold in colour. It is a popular metal for silversmiths to practise with as, other than the colour, it acts in a similar way to silver when being formed.

ALUMINIUM

A white metal element, aluminium is light and can be hard or annealed. It is sometimes cast. It can be polished to a very bright state but dulls fairly quickly. Specialist aluminium solders are available. Its relatively low melting point of 660°C (1220°C) makes it tricky to join, but it is this quality that makes it popular for casting decorative objects.

It can be hard to colour and, as noted above, the shine dulls quickly unless there is some sort of coating applied to it, such as paint or lacquer. I polish it in the same way that I polish silver.

LEAD

This is a heavy, soft, grey element. Everyone is aware of the hazards of lead. Care must be taken when using any products containing lead. Heat it only in a well-ventilated area, and wash your hands thoroughly after using it.

It can be handy as a support for smaller pieces when it is cast into a container. The hockey-puck-shaped result is called a 'lead cake', and is used as a backing for stamping or punching.

Some solders contain lead and previous repairs on an item may have been made using lead solder. It is important to recognize when a soft solder repair has been previously made, as future repairs will need to made in the same way to avoid burning the silver away.

IMPORTANT

The smallest amount of lead – just a pin prick – on the surface of silver heated to annealing/silver soldering temperatures will burn a hole through the surface! Many silversmiths will not allow lead into their workshop for this reason.

SECRETS OF LEAD

• To help avoid accidental lead burns on precious pieces, have a separate marked kiln shelf (soldering surface) for soft solders, kept away from the normal silver soldering surface. I mark mine with a big 'L'.

TIN

Tin is a silvery element with a low melting point of 232°C (450°F). It is often combined with other elements to produce alloys such as pewter and bronze. It is also used to plate or cover iron or steel to stop it corroding – 'tin' cans are actually steel with a covering of tin. This makes it food safe and stops it rusting.

When decorative objects are coated in tin like this, they are often called 'tin-plate'. Many toys were made from tin plate; it behaves like steel when you work on it. Tin plate toys can be brittle and snap if parts are overworked. It is easy to soft solder when carrying out repairs.

IRON AND STEEL

Iron is an element and steel is an alloy of iron. Most tools are made from these materials. It can be welded, brazed or riveted to join two bits together. It can be made hard for tools such as drills and chisels, or soft as in cast-iron or mild steel, or for example binding wire. Iron has a melting point of 1538°C (2800°F).

Iron and steel will polish. There are specialist compounds for this, but I use Tripoli and rouge, the same compounds (see page 44) that I use for silver. I keep my hammers and stakes polished in this way.

WHITE METAL

White metal is a general term for alloys made from tin, zinc, antimony, cadmium and bismuth. White metal is a catch-all term that encompass products including pewter, spelter, Britannia metal and pot metal. Many decorative objects are made from these alloys. They all have a low melting point – as low as 170°C (338°F) – and are therefore easy to cast and manipulate.

There are many examples of white metal described here; this jug is a typical illustration of a white metal piece.

Britannia metal Not to be confused with Britannia silver, the composition by weight of this white metal is about 92% tin, 6% antimony and 2% copper. It melts at around 255°C (491°F). A silver-plated Britannia metal item may have the stamp EPBM (electro-plated Britannia metal) stamped on it. It is soft when filed and can clog a file. It can be soldered – but only very carefully, and with a low melting temperature solder. It is a risky procedure and much practice should be done with an expendable piece before trying to solder something important.

Pewter The various forms of this alloy melt between 170°C (338°F) and 300°C (572°F). Unfortunately, without expensive specialist equipment, it is impossible to know what mixture the alloy is, and it is therefore very hard to determine the exact melting point. To help avoid this, English pewter is standardized at 91% tin, 7.5% antimony and 1.5% copper, and has a melting point of 250°C (482°F).

German Silver or Nickel Silver The usual composition by weight of this white metal is about 60% copper, 20% nickel and 20% zinc. It melts at around 1100°C (2012°F).

Spelter Commonly used to fashion objects such as sculptures, clock cases and lamps, spelter is a zinc/lead alloy which was historically employed as a type of 'budget' bronze. It has a far lower melting temperature than bronze, which meant the furnaces used were cheaper to run and the resulting metal was more affordable.

If you scratch or scape through the patina or coating of a spelter object, the metal will appear silver or grey in colour, whereas bronze is a gold colour. If it is tapped, spelter has a duller ring than bronze. It is also more brittle and more likely to show scratches and dents as it is more susceptible to damage than a bronze item.

Due to its lead content, a mask should be worn when working on spelter and you should always wash your hands well after work.

SECRETS OF WHITE METAL

- *Many white metals contain lead, with the associated dangers. I recommend that white metal soldering repairs are carried out on a different soldering block/kiln shelf to the ones that silver are soldered on to help avoid potential lead contamination.*
- *White metals can be painted, polished, plated to look like silver, or patinated to look like bronze.*
- *Great care needs to be taken when trying to solder items made with these materials if you don't want to end up with a pool of molten metal on your hearth!*

WHAT IS A HALLMARK?

A hallmark is a set of component marks applied to articles of the precious metals gold, silver, platinum or palladium. The presence of a hallmark means that the article has been independently tested, and it guarantees that it conforms to all legal standards of purity (fineness). It also guarantees the item's provenance by telling us where the piece was hallmarked, what the article is made from, and who sent the article for hallmarking.

The picture above shows me striking my sponsor's mark as the finishing touch to a new piece, prior to sending it to the Assay Office for testing. It will then receive the Sterling standard, town and date stamps.

HISTORY OF HALLMARKING

Pure or 'fine' silver (marked 999) is too soft to make objects for everyday use. It was found that by mixing other metal elements with silver, the lustre remained but the metal was much harder and more durable. However, the amount of these added metals varied. This meant no one knew how much (in percentage terms) an item was actually pure silver. That is to say, the silver could be 'watered down' by cheaper non-precious metals.

As early as 1238, King Henry III of England tried to set a standard for precious metals. It was important that an independent body tested and stamped items to prevent fraud. By testing and stamping, people knew the quality of what they were buying. This was a very early form of trading standards and offered consumers protection from fraud and guaranteed value for money. Metal quality testing methods had developed and were accurate. In around 1300 Edward I decreed that no piece of silver 'was to depart out of the hands of the workers' until it had been 'assayed' (which is taken from the French word for test) and marked with a leopard's head. Sterling silver should be 925 parts silver per 1,000 – or to put it another way, 92.5%.

Over the years the marks have changed and evolved. For example, Each Assay Office has (or had) its own individual identifying stamp and fonts for the date letters, which change each year. Happily, many of these marks, including all the date letters, are well documented. With some research you can tell where and when an object was made and by whom. With a little bit of knowledge, it can be easily ascertained what is a genuine UK precious metal object.

HALLMARKS AND THE LAW

It is against the law in the course of a trade or business to sell or describe precious metal articles in the UK that are un-hallmarked and above the weight exemptions. So for example, a silver item weighing less than 7.78 grams would not need to be hallmarked but could be still described as silver. Trading Standards Officers have the power to seize any items that do not comply with the 1973 Hallmarking Act, which can lead to prosecution and a fine of up to £5,000 per article.

As an anecdote, when I was training as a silversmith in the 1970s, an item that I had spent eight weeks making (a pen and ink box) failed assay by a tiny fraction of a percent. I had been sold sub-standard silver by a supplier. The rules then were that the item had to be destroyed. It arrived back hammered flat. Thankfully, if a piece of precious metals fails assay today, the Assay Office can mark it at a lower standard. They still have the right to destroy the item but this rarely happens.

 London*   Edinburgh*   Birmingham*

 Chester   Dublin   Sheffield*

 Exeter   Glasgow   Newcastle

Hallmarking in the UK

Hallmarking is the marking of a precious metal item after it has been assayed by a regulated body in the UK run by the Goldsmith's Hall. Although in the past some regional towns and cities, including Dublin, had Assay Offices, today just four Assay Offices remain in the UK: London, Birmingham, Sheffield and Edinburgh – these are marked with an asterisk above.

The UK has been a signatory to the International Convention on Hallmarks (see below) since its inception in 1972.

Hallmarking across the world

The Convention on the Control and Marking (CCM) of Articles of Precious Metals (known as the Hallmarking Convention) is an international treaty between Contracting States, which aims to eliminate trade barriers in the cross-border trade of precious metal articles. Signed in Vienna on the 15th of November 1972, the Convention came into force in 1975. Its text was mainly drafted and negotiated in Geneva and London, and Goldsmiths' Hall is widely considered the Convention's 'birth place'.

In the United States and Australia there are no government Assay Offices. Instead, there are trading standards and various guilds and associations that set a standard for their members.

ANATOMY OF A HALLMARK

Hallmarks vary a great deal. In the UK, the compulsory elements are the sponsor's mark (sometimes called a maker's mark) and the Assay Office town mark. The other elements are optional.

The example below, from the UK, shows the sort of hallmark you might find on an article. Even without seeing the object, we can tell that it is made from sterling silver by Brenton West, and was assayed in London in 2022.

Sponsor's mark	Metal fineness mark	Assay Office town mark	Date letter

Sponsor's mark This indicates who submitted the article for hallmarking, and is unique to the maker. This example shown above is my own. It contains my initials with a unique border. There will never be another CBW metalsmith with this particular surround.

Metal fineness mark This shows what the article is made of. The lion in an octagonal box is a traditional marking that means sterling silver, while the 925 in an oval is a 'millesimal fineness mark', a numerical format that became compulsory in 1999. It expresses the precious metal content in parts per thousand.

Assay Office town mark Where the item was hallmarked.

Date letter When the item was hallmarked.

Commemorative marks

On very special state occasions the Assay Offices offer a commemorative mark, which is placed next to the date letter of the hallmark. This examples above are commemorative marks to celebrate the coronation of King Charles III (above left) and the Platinum Jubilee of Queen Elizabeth II (above right).

Pictured here are my stamps, registered at and made by The London Assay Office in 1977. Note that one is cranked (bent) to allow it to manoeuvre within and stamp the inside of rings.

MAKING YOUR MARK: PUNCHES

A hallmark is traditionally struck using a stamp. The sponsor's mark is made by the Assay Office to a unique design that is never changed with those initials. The maker stamps his or her own stamp before sending the item for testing. When adding the sponsor's mark, extreme concentration is required, as one slip-up and the punch will damage the finished item irreparably.

When the Assay Office receives the item, it is tested using X-ray fluorescence spectrometry (XRF). This digitally reads the composition of the metal alloy very accurately. The remainder of the stamps applied by the Assay Office are either applied by using stamps or a less invasive laser stamp can be requested. The advantage of the latter is that the metal is not distorted by the application of a laser mark. The downside is the laser marks are much shallower than struck marks and are best suited inside an object where they are less likely to be worn away.

RECOGNIZING A GENUINE HALLMARK

Care must be taken before attempting to repair an item to define whether it is 'solid' silver or whether it is plated. Plating is a covering of silver over a cheaper 'base' metal. This covering or plate can be worn through by over-polishing or by the actions of the repair that you are about to attempt. Before you attempt a repair, It is important to know whether you are going to need the facilities to re-plate the item after working on it.

It is illegal to copy hallmarks, but plated items often have marks designed to look like hallmarks to the casual observer, so that they appear to be sterling silver. A silver-plated item's marks need to be studied to confirm its status. Silver-plated items are often made with EPNS (electro-plated nickel silver), EP (electro-plated) or EPBM (electro-plated Britannia metal).

Sheffield plate is another form of a silver covering where silver sheet is fused to copper with heat and rolled to the desired thickness for working. This was invented in the sixteenth century. Electro-plating took over from Sheffield plate and was all but superseded in the mid-nineteenth century by electro-plating. Sheffield plate can be electro-plated after repair.

It should be noted that some of these marks try to emulate 'original' Assay Office hallmarks and it is important to be aware of the differences. This helps you avoid buying an item that is not the genuine precious metal that it purports to be.

An example of marks indicating electro-plated Britannia metal.

Two examples of marks that clearly state the item is plated.

Unknown marks, likely intended to resemble hallmarks.

SILVERSMITH'S SECRET

Don't be put off by the notes above – there are many fine plated items which can be amazing value for money. They are excellent to practise on – or to use and display.

Tools

At root, the tools that any repairer needs are ones that will do the job. Often, general-purpose tools you have lying around the house such as hammers, pliers or files can be enough to carry out a repair. With that said, specialist tools are often much better, as each one is designed to do a very particular job.

I always buy the most expensive tools that I can afford at the time of purchase. Some of my tools are forty-five years old and still going strong. There are many budget tools available that are not precisely made, and are of poor quality. These are sure to fail.

The following pages look at which tools are absolutely essential for the silversmith's workshop, and those which are beyond the basic but remain extremely useful. These are labelled as shown to the right.

Essential

Core tools or equipment that all silversmiths require.

Specialist

Useful to have as an extra option, or for particular specialist tasks.

HAMMERS

Even a basic tool set should include a variety of hammers. A craftsman never has enough tools! What is important is to work out how one balances the desire to own forty hammers and the actual necessity of owning forty hammers. Personally, I have around fifteen hammers and it is rare that I need any other shapes or designs.

Keep the faces of your hammers polished so any taps on metal make smooth, shiny marks.

SILVERSMITHING HAMMERS

The following silversmithing hammers are useful as they can get in to areas that other hammers cannot reach:

Doming hammer The most useful of all, to my mind, doming hammers have half convex sphere ends that make them useful for knocking dents from spoons. If highly polished, they are also useful for burnishing dents from objects.

Creasing hammer Quite thin-edged, these hammers are used for adding a textured finish and for getting into those 'hard to get at' places.

Raising hammer A hammer with a flat face and a right-angled edge with a small radius, it is used for raising flat silver discs into bowls, vases, decanters and so forth. It is a very useful hammer for certain repairs.

Collet hammer Similar to a raising hammer, collet hammers have a slightly different profile and a longer reach.

Silversmithing hammers

From left to right: doming hammer, creasing hammer, raising hammer, collet hammer.

Planishing hammers
The detail (below right) shows the highly-polished faces of the planishing hammers.

PLANISHING HAMMERS

These are the most useful hammers in the silversmith's armoury. They are used with a supporting stake behind for smoothing metal, and can also be used as a burnisher.

Flat-headed These are used for planishing, straightening and smoothing.

Round- or dome-headed Excellent for knocking dents out of concave and curved surfaces.

Square hammer Useful to get access into boxes. Many planishing hammers have both a round and a square end.

SECRETS OF HAMMERS

On occasion, I re-shape or re-fashion the face of some of my hammers for certain situations:

- *You will note a 'half-headed' planishing hammer above. I had to cut this to fit inside a small box. It felt wrong to cut a tool, but it has since proved a really useful addition to my toolbox – in fact, it's now one of my favourites.*
- *A piece I was repairing had irreplaceable engraving that meant I could not mark the metal in any way. To remove a dent without marking the metal, I taped a piece of leather to the face of a yellow-headed hammer (a plastic hard hammer), and used this to carefully knock out the dent. You can see this temporary adaptation in the picture opposite.*

Mallets and other hammers
From left to right: nylon mallet, hide mallet, chasing hammer, doming mallet, pin hammer, plastic mallet, jeweller's hammer/mallet.

MALLETS AND OTHER HAMMERS

Mallets differ from hammers in that they have non-metallic heads.

Soft hide or leather mallets Made from leather, this is useful for striking metal without marking it as much as using a metal hammer. They are quite large so not good for intricate detailed work.

Hard nylon mallets Again, another useful option to use to hit metal without leaving too many marks.

Doming mallet As the name suggests, these are used for forming larger dome shapes; good for bowls.

Pin hammer Used for hitting small veneer or panel pins into wood. Not to be used on metal, as the face will have marks left by the nails that it has struck – and those marks will be imparted onto the surface.

Chasing hammer Used for hitting small punches, its large face makes hitting the small target easier.

Jeweller's hammer A small, lightweight hammer perfect for precision work.

Snarling iron

SNARLING IRON

Not a hammer, but always used with one; snarling irons are essential for removing dents in items when hands simply cannot reach inside. A snarling iron is a long metal bar with a little springy 'give' in it. One end is clamped in a vice to secure it. The other end is smooth, polished and has the profile of the item to be repaired. By hitting the metal bar, the 'business end' springs back up and knocks out the dent from the inside.

PIERCING SAW

Sometimes known as a jeweller's saw, a piercing saw is a delicate adjustable saw frame. It is designed to cut material while causing as little waste as possible. The blades cut on the down stroke and, once mastered, amazing shapes and detail can be cut with them.

Blades Saw blades are available usually by the dozen. Assortment packs are also available. These selections are useful to test out which blades you get on with and also to test out certain circumstances when you are met with various materials.

- Blades range from 8/0, which is the very finest, down through to 1/0, then they rise up to 4 (see table opposite).

- I always buy expensive, usually Swiss, quality blades. They last longer and are more likely to cut straight than the cheap ones.

Piercing saw and blades

The detail below shows 6/0 (top) and 4 (bottom) saw blades. A ruler with millimetres is shown for scale.

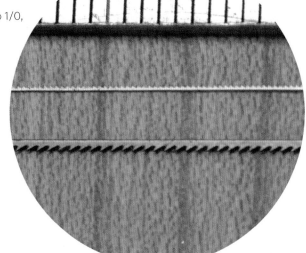

SILVERSMITH'S SECRET

I always saw as though the blade is about to break, imagining where the broken part will bury itself in my finger. This has stood me in good stead so far. I have avoided injury by being mindful of this (thankfully quite rare) potential accident.

Saw blade specification	Blade thickness (mm)	Blade width (mm)	Blade length (mm)	Teeth per cm	Corresponding drill size (mm)	Suitable metal gauge (mm)
Grade 4	0.38	0.8	130	15	0.8	1.0–1.3
Grade 3	0.36	0.74	130	16	0.8	0.9–1.2
Grade 2	0.34	0.7	130	17.5	0.7	0.9–1.1
Grade 1	0.3	0.63	130	19	0.7	0.8–1.0
Grade 0 (1/0)	0.28	0.58	130	20.5	0.6	0.6–0.95
Grade 2/0	0.26	0.52	130	22	0.55	0.6–0.8
Grade 3/0	0.24	0.48	130	23.5	0.5	0.6–0.7
Grade 4/0	0.22	0.44	130	26.5	0.5	0.5–0.6
Grade 5/0	0.2	0.4	130	28	0.4	0.4–0.55
Grade 6/0	0.18	0.35	130	32	0.4	0.35–0.5
Grade 8/0	0.17	0.3	130	30	0.3	Up to 0.4

SNIPS

I rarely use snips or 'tin snips' as they are sometimes called, preferring a piercing saw to cut metal. Snips come in handy sometimes and are relatively cheap to purchase.

Snips

From left to right: left curve, right curve and straight cut.

PLIERS

Like hammers, you simply cannot have too many pairs of pliers.

Ring pliers (A) Curved on one face and flat on the other, these are for forming curves in metal (tubular), and rings.

Round tapered pliers (B) These are for bending smaller round pieces.

Flat-nosed (C) and snipe-nosed pliers (D) Both of these are used for gripping material.

Parallel action pliers (E) Cleverly designed, the faces remain parallel as they open and close. This means that a piece can be gripped along the whole face of the pliers. The advantages of this are that these pliers grip much better than ordinary action pliers and secondly, they are less likely to damage the work, as a large surface area is gripping the piece of silver.

Side cutters (F) Fine side cutters are used for precious metal wire, while strong side cutters are used for thicker wire and iron binding wire.

Pallion cutting snips (G) Designed for cutting sheet solder (see pages 41 and 61 for more) accurately, these are a useful luxury, but not essential.

A
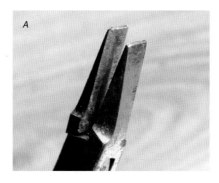

B

C

D
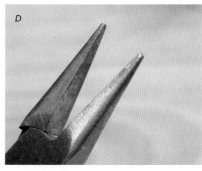

E

F
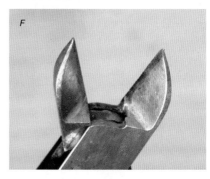

G

MEASURING AND MARKING TOOLS

These tools are essential to effect a proper repair:

Scriber and dividers Used for marking lines on work, the dividers make arcs and circles easy.

Vernier gauge A device to measure thickness; a digital one is handy. Keep a spare battery, though – it is useless if the battery goes flat; mine seems to do so just when I really need it to work!

Dixième gauge Handy for measuring the thickness of items when a Vernier gauge cannot be used. See page 78 for more on this handy tool.

Straight edge Used for marking and checking straight lines.

Centre-punch Used to make indentations in metal, particularly marking the centre of a hole as a guide for drilling.

Square Used for checking that an object is square – or more broadly, checking and marking angles.

Measuring and marking tools

Clockwise from top left: dividers, Vernier gauge, three centre-punches, engineer's square, straight edge, odd leg calliper's, dixième gauge.

ODD LEG CALLIPERS

These enable a parallel line to be scribed along the edge of material. Very much a luxury.

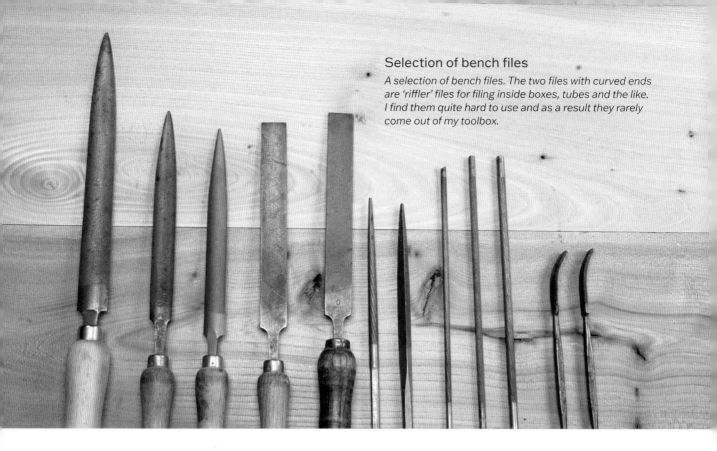

A selection of bench files. The two files with curved ends are 'riffler' files for filing inside boxes, tubes and the like. I find them quite hard to use and as a result they rarely come out of my toolbox.

FILES AND ABRASIVES

There are a multitude of files with varying degrees of cutting coarseness. The key ones are larger bench files (also known as engineer's files) and smaller needle files. The texture and coarseness of a file is referred to as their 'cut'.

Keep files in a cloth roll or in their package to stop them rubbing together. This will save them from wearing each other out unnecessarily.

BENCH FILES

Bench files are available in various shapes including flat, half round, and three square (triangular). one of my favourites, the crossing file, is similar to a half-round file but has a flatter, gentler curve on one side and a deeper curve on the other. It used to be called a 'fishback', due to its shape.

WET AND DRY PAPER

There's only so much you can do with files, so when you need to smooth a surface beyond their capabilities, reach for these:

Wet and dry paper Waterproof paper made from silicon carbide grit with grades from around 80/7000. The silversmith's workshop would typically use a range of grades between 240 to 3000. The glue and paper are water resistant and these papers can be used wet very effectively. The water can help to clear the abrasive from blocking up and slows blunting of the grit.

Water of Ayr stone A natural slate-like stone used to smooth metal after filing and wet and dry sanding. It is used wet. It is no longer available 'new', but it turns up on auction sites.

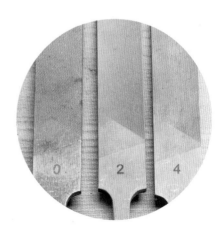

File cuts
This detail shows three flat files with grades 0, 2, and 4. The lower the grade, the more abrasive the file is. Work up the grades from coarse to smooth.

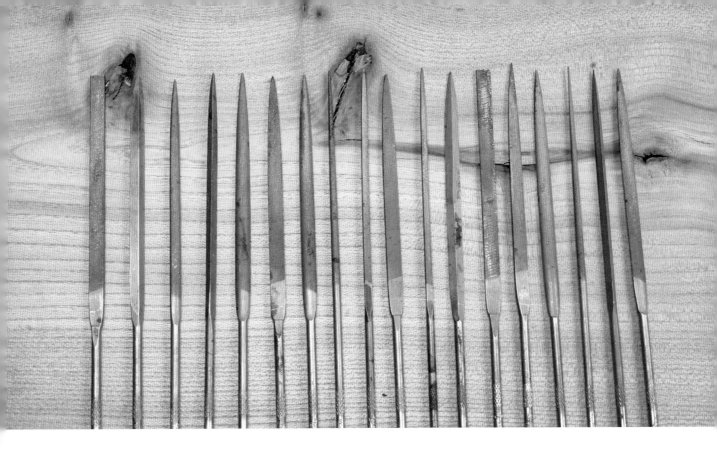

🔧 NEEDLE FILES

Available in different grades, fine- or medium-cut are preferable. A single set will suffice. Specialist needle files are also available in different cuts.

Needle files, fine and medium

A good set of needle files is expensive, but if looked after will last for a long time.

SECRETS OF FILES

- *When I buy a set of needle files, I mark the handles with a coloured paint – red in the example – to distinguish medium files from fine files. This way I can tell at a glance which set they are from.*
- *Both round parallel chainsaw files and flat raker files are great value and give a coarse cut. Intended for chainsaw chains, they are available from garden machinery retailers.*

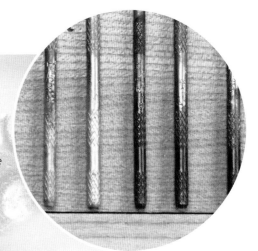

SOLDERING TOOLS

TORCH

Soldering is a key element of silversmithing. A torch of some sort is essential, but what you need will depend on what you intend to repair. A lighter gas torch or propane torch is essential; the others are luxuries.

Propane torch A basic propane torch set-up is the most versatile method of heating; a small bottle can be used, which will not take up too much space. Nozzles vary in size so that you can do fine work as well as heating big items such as teapots. A kit can be purchased that has the handle, hose and gas regulator. Extra nozzles are also available.

Lighter gas torch The very smallest lighter gas torch can be used for small jewellery repairs and soft solder repairs on larger items where the whole object does not need to be heated up. These torches would not be hot enough to silver solder larger items.

Oxy propane/propylene torch For the more advanced user, these mix oxygen and a gas inside the torch to make flames that vary from a micro flame, fantastic for intricate work, right up to one capable of cutting steel. The torches themselves vary in size, but the bottles, gauges and flashback arrestors are universal.

Propane torch set
Extra nozzles are shown to the left.

Small lighter-gas torch
This example is self-igniting. Great for browning off food in the kitchen, too!

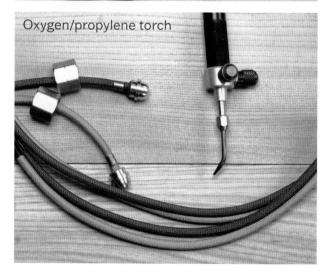

Oxygen/propylene torch

SOLDERING ACCESSORIES

Tungsten probe Used for manipulating solder when heating. Tungsten melts at a much higher temperature, so is unaffected.

Flux and accessories Usually containing borax (for hard soldering), flux helps to keep a joint clean and enables the solder to flow into a joint once molten. Other fluxes are used for soft soldering. The most common flux, borax, is sold in a cone. It is rubbed in a ceramic dish with water to make a paste which is then painted onto the cleaned joint with a paintbrush prior to soldering. You can read more about flux on page 60.

Tweezers Used to place or hold pallions of solder (see page 61) while you work. Reverse-action tweezers open only when you squeeze them, so they can also hold or support small items, leaving both hands free.

Pickle pot *(not pictured)* Pickle is a liquid compound that removes flux and oxidation from jewellery after soldering. Bought as granules that are dissolved in water, pickle solution works when warm. A budget slow cooker is a great cost saving and can be used as a pickle pot – obviously, it is not to be used in the kitchen afterwards!

Solder *(pictured on page 61)* A soft fusible metal alloy that is melted to secure metals together. The various types are explained in more detail on page 61.

Soldering accessories
Clockwise from top left: tungsten probe, borax dish, borax cone, pallion cutting snips (see page 36), various tweezers, paintbrush.

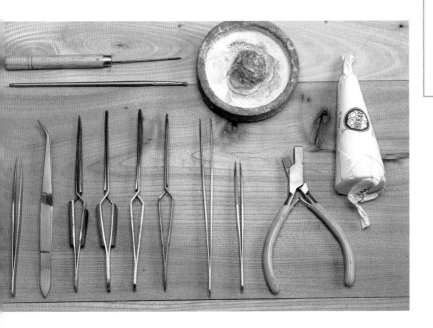

Engraving tools
Small chisel, engravers and Arkansas sharpening stone.

ENGRAVERS AND CHISELS

Used for cleaning away solder from tight areas, engravers/gravers are also useful for creating 'stiches' – slightly raised punctuations in the silver that you can use to hold the piece in place while you solder it. If you become proficient at engraving, old worn engraving can be enhanced.

They should be kept sharp so they are less likely to slip when cutting. The stone also pictured is used for sharpening. Resources are available online for these specialist skills.

SUPPORTING SURFACES

It is necessary to have a flat plate of some sort for truing and levelling (see page 71), and a flat heatproof surface is also necessary for soldering.

Engineer's surface plate Available in various materials, the key thing is that it is absolutely flat and level.

Surface gauge An adjustable holder for a scriber. This has a flat base that sits on the surface plate, as pictured to the right.

Potter's decoration wheel and accessories Work often needs to be rotated to deliver an even heat to the whole object – a potter's decoration wheel is a robust cast iron wheel with a good bearing, and is ideal for these purposes. The wheel has concentric rings marked on it so that you can be sure to get your item centred.

Pottery kiln shelves A kiln shelf is a ceramic sheet around 20mm (¾in) thick, able to withstand enormous temperatures. Available from pottery suppliers, they can be used for soldering on and can be useful behind an area where flames are directed. Separate shelf supports are also handy for balancing and supporting items.

Firebricks Small heatproof blocks, these are used to support small items while being heated, or to raise items from the surface.

Surface plate and surface gauge

Potter's decoration wheel
Also pictured are a kiln shelf (right) and spacers (on top of the wheel).

LEATHER SAND BAG

Used for resting a piece on while working on it, a leather sand bag is relatively firm, but the surface of the leather is forgiving and does not damage the silver that you might lay on it.

Leather sand bag

My first sand bag sprang a leak after forty years. I patched it for a while, but this is now my second and final sand bag.

BENCH AND BENCH SKIN

Although a bespoke bench is not a requirement, it is a great thing to have. With a half round cut-out, you can keep your tools around you as you work. You also have a leather skin that hooks under the cut-out in the bench. Your knees slide under the bench skin as you work, and it will catch precious metal lemel, tools and small items when you drop them.

The skin can be made by buying a hide and adding brass eyes where necessary.

Bench with cut-out and leather skin

This leather skin is suspended under the cut-out above the worker's knees. The wooden 'bench-peg' is the centre of operations.

POLISHING MOTOR, MOPS AND COMPOUNDS

Polishing motor A polishing motor comes with a threaded tapered spindle that the mops screw onto. The spindles are sided, that is, a right-hand thread on the right and a left-hand thread on left. This ensures that the mop always tightens itself onto the machine when it is rotating. I have always only used the right-hand side of my polishing motor. An extractor should be fitted.

Mops Mops are rotary brushes made from various materials, most commonly cotton. They are stitched onto a leather boss attached to the spindle of the polishing motor. Felts are hard buffing mops, with tapered felt for polishing the inside of rings. You cannot switch compounds on mops, so I spray red paint on the sides of rouge mops to avoid ruining them by adding the more abrasive Tripoli compound to them by mistake.

Compounds Many types of compounds are available. I was trained to used Tripoli compound and rouge for the final polish. Tripoli is a fine abrasive suspended in a waxy substance. It is used for removing fine scratches from the metal surface. Rouge is fine iron oxide, again often supplied in a waxy bar. Finer than Tripoli compound, it is used for the final polish.

Polishing motor with mop fitted

I have owned this motor for over forty years. It has a home-made removable cover with a Perspex see-through top (just visible at the top of the picture). There is a home-made extractor below the work bench.

Mops, brushes and compounds

Pictured here are mops, felts and brushes, which are for polishing and finishing the inside of round hollow vessels. At the bottom are Tripoli and rouge compound. Both are cheap and have worked for me and countless other metalsmiths for years, so I see no reason to change to more modern compounds. Feel free to experiment, though.

VICE

A device to hold items firmly in place, a large bench vice is necessary to hold stakes while working on an item. I prefer a quick release vice, with a lever enabling the jaws to be drawn apart without winding the tee bar incessantly. A smaller engineer's vice is also useful for smaller jobs at the bench.

Moveable engineer's bench vice

STAKES

Used as formers to shape metal over, the stake supports the work while manipulating, usually with a hammer or mallet. Stakes can be made from cast iron, steel, brass or even wood. They are the backbone of a silversmith's workshop.

Each stake needs to be designed to fit the bespoke job for which it is going to be used, so bear this in mind: you don't need a stake until you know what stake you need. It is pretty pointless buying a set of stakes, some of which will never be used. It is best to buy or make stakes as required.

Stakes

This collection contains some of the stakes that I have acquired and made over the years.

BURNISHERS AND SCRAPERS

Burnishers are used to remove dents or deep scratches from metal. Deep scratches can be burnished out and unwanted solder can be scraped with a scraper.

Some burnishers are bought but you can make them from old files – just heat them, bend and polish them. The metal is high quality and excellent for re-using once the file is blunt.

Scrapers and burnishers

DOMING BLOCK AND PUNCHES

Used in concert with the doming block, punches are used to make curves and domes in sheet metal. You can buy ready-made sets.

The doming punches are good for pushing dents out, either by tapping or using as a burnisher.

Doming block and punches

SECRETS OF PUNCHES

I sometimes use brass to make punches. It is quick to fashion and easy to polish, and although not hugely durable as a punch, it is certainly good enough for two or three jobs, which is often all they're needed for.

PITCH PAN AND PITCH

Used for melting pitch to re-fill filled silver items (see pages 114 and 121) – and if you're planning to do so, you can count this as an essential – all you need is a cheap pan from the discount store. It will work really well.

Small pieces of pine resin pitch are broken off with a hammer, and can then be heated in the pan with a paint stripper hot-air gun until they melt, ready for use.

Pitch and pitch pan

DRILLS

Cordless hand drill
This is useful for drilling holes – and for home DIY!

Pendant drill Used for polishing small items and reaching in difficult areas, for years I used a flexible shaft motor that was single (high) speed and hand-switched. This was very useful, but not hugely controllable. I acquired the pictured foot-operated, variable speed, quick-release chuck pendant drill a few years ago. I survived for years without it – now I couldn't live without it!

Cordless hand drill

Pendant drill

Flexible shaft pendant drill with foot-operated pedal. There are a myriad of attachments available that insert into the chuck of the pendant drill handle. These include drills, burrs, buffs, grinders, brass and steel wire-wheels, cutters and sanders.

⚙ SILVER-PLATING EQUIPMENT

Essential if you intend to repair plated goods (see pages 72–73). If you are only going to be repairing sterling silver, then plating equipment is unnecessary.

Power supply Low voltage DC – you won't get a shock! Two cables, one positive, one negative, are attached to the power supply.

Plating electrodes A wand-like device with a swab or brush that is attached to the positive cable.

Silver salt solution Sold in bottles as silver-plating solution, this is an electrolyte – a liquid with dissolved ions of silver.

Silver-plating kit

⚙ ROLLING MILL

If you need a certain thickness or gauge of metal for a job, it can be ordered from your silver suppliers – the disadvantage is that you have to wait for it to come. You can instead run silver wire or sheet through the milling wheels to flatten it to the exact thickness you need.

If you are melting down scrap silver (see opposite) to re-fashion into sheet or wire, a rolling mill becomes essential.

Rolling mill
Basic models like this come up second-hand every now and then, so keep an eye out.

SCRAP CONTAINER

Most important. Keep all of the filings and cuttings that are produced when working on precious metals. You can melt down this scrap (known as lemel) and re-fashion it yourself, or weigh it in and sell it – the return can be substantial.

Scrap container
There is approximately a 1kg (2lb 3oz) of scrap here – it soon adds up.

TUBE HOLDER

Used for cutting, this is a luxury in general, but if hinges are being repaired it is essential. The chenier has to have a flat face at a right angle to the tube for the hinge to work. Once the tube is cut, it can be filed in the holder to ensure this.

Commercial, very sophisticated ones are available some with forty-five-degree options. These are useful for cutting small pieces of sheet metal at that angle.

Tube holder
I made this tube cutter as a college project.

HAND BRUSHES

Effective when used wet, brass brushes are used for cleaning textured, chased or patterned surfaces that have not got a flat polished surface.

The black and white brushes pictured here are a pair, used with cleaner chemicals on metal objects. The bristles of the black brush are hard and those of the white brush soft.

The file brush can help remove clogged files.

Hand brushes
From left to right: file brush, small hard-bristle brush, brass brushes in two different sizes, hard-bristle brush, soft-bristle brush and small brass brush.

ULTRASOUND CLEANER

With the right chemicals mixed with water, this ultrasound cleaner is great for cleaning in those hard-to-reach places. It works by heating the water and vibrates at a high frequency, shaking the dirt off any item placed within. Fingers should not enter the bath when the machine is active.

It also removes polish residue which can be quite stubborn at times. It is a handy bit of kit. I have got by without one for years but finally succumbed and bought one about a year ago.

Ultrasonic cleaner

Two-part epoxy adhesive
This particular type is JB Weld. Mix the two components evenly on a piece of scrap.

Two-part epoxy putty
This is Milliput, prior to mixing.

ADHESIVES

Protective gloves should be used when using adhesives, especially two-part epoxy resins.

JB Weld For repairing metal, the best product to connect joints is JB Weld. It is a two-part epoxy and is very strong when used according to the manufacturers' instructions.

Araldite For repairing wood there are a number of adhesives. A two-part epoxy resin such as Araldite is good for broken handles (used with a splint) as it is very strong.

PVA Larger wood repairs require PVA wood glue where there is a greater surface area to bond to.

Super glue This is a very strong quick-setting adhesive, based on cyanoacrylates. It can be handy in the right circumstance. It can be brittle. It is hard to reverse so great care should be used using super glues. Activators are available in an aerosol that make super glues set instantly.

SILVERSMITH'S SECRET

Always make sure that any joint is snug-fitting and clean. Generally speaking, the less glue the better. Always try to clamp the pieces together when gluing.

FILLERS

Repairs often require some filling to make the area uniform before re-colouring. A mask should be worn when sanding all fillers. There are two types:

Two-part epoxy putty The two parts are mixed together and can then be moulded into shapes or used to fill gaps where a repair has been joined. The putty then cures and hardens. I recommend Milliput.

Two-part polyester fillers These are quick setting and easy to sand for final filling operations. Wood filler and car body filler are both quite similar and both useful for wood and metal. For very fine filling operations, such as file marks, I recommend two-part 'stopper', available from car accessory merchants. This shouldn't be used for filling large voids.

SECRETS OF MILLIPUT

- A gloved finger can be moistened to help smooth the putty.
- It is slow to set, so there is plenty of time to make sure that the filling is correct to the profile of the item being filled.
- It can be filed or sanded, and it can be coloured with paint.

MATERIALS AND TOOLS FOR FINISHING

Wood finishes After any sanding operations following a repair, French polish can be applied with a tightly wadded soft cloth, moving in gentle strokes, allowing the polish to set before adding another coat. It brings out the colour and grain in a tired wooden handle or base. Once the French polish is completely dry, it can be 'denibbed' using 0000 wire wool. Then a good quality furniture polish can be applied and buffed with a soft cloth to bring out the shine.

Metal finishes Apart from a polished finish, metals can have a coating or patina which needs to be matched after repair. Silver can be blackened or aged with Liver of Sulphur, while copper and brass can be blackened or aged with metal colouring called Tourmaline.

Wax polish Renaissance wax polish is a microcrystalline wax, developed for conservation by the British Museum. It can be applied to just about any object to protect it, giving a fine barrier against tarnish or damage. There are other wax polishes available – look for a high-quality brand.

Lacquer There are many lacquers that can be applied to metal to protect it and stop it tarnishing. It can be applied by brush or by spray. It is important that the metal is clean and grease free before applying lacquer. It is an appropriate finish for complex decorative items that are rarely handled. If lacquer is worn or chipped off, tarnish can set in and the surface may look uneven. Fortunately, lacquer can always be removed with the correct solvent. Do not be afraid of working on a patchy half-lacquered item, as you can strip it off.

Having used good-quality silver polish to hand-buff the silver of this coffee pot, I'm using Fiddes wax polish to bring the wooden handle back to a bright sheen.
You can see the full repair project on pages 142–147.

OTHER USEFUL EQUIPMENT

Perhaps less glamorous and exciting than the other tools, these are nevertheless important.

Cleaning pens Useful to clean in corners prior to soldering, these retractable pens hold either replaceable brass or glass fibre inserts. As the end wears out, the insert is advanced a bit. Note that the fibreglass bits break as the tool is being used and become very intense itching powder – I recommend a mask and gloves if using this pen.

Binding wire Made from mild steel, and available in coils or reels, binding wire is invaluable for a number of uses, from holding parts together during a repair to keeping an object elevated from the kiln shelf while soldering.

Clamps *(not pictured)* Clamps are essential for holding larger objects together during repairs.

Lathe *(not pictured)* A luxury non-essential item, a lathe is a machine that holds metal and makes it rotate. By working a sharpened tool into the metal, it can be shaped, reduced in size or drilled.

Binding wire

Cleaning pens

*Left to right: brass and glass fibre tips.
The inserts are cheap to replace.*

Planning and preparing

Whatever you are repairing, determination and tenacity will be required: things won't always go well. If a repair fails, step back and work out why. Leave it for a while before going back, consider your new approach. More often than not you will find that you have missed a process out or maybe you tried to cut a corner. The item will always catch you out if you aren't observing the due process for it.

It is important to have confidence in the core skills described on the following pages before tackling any repair on a precious or irreplaceable item.

ASSESSING

This is perhaps the most important part of the job, and essential prior to beginning any repair work, as assessing the object will help you to plan what tools and techniques you need to repair it.

Look at the object and its fault, and ask yourself how it became damaged. Was it a trauma? Or simply wear and tear? Why is it broken or damaged? If a hinge is broken, was it because the lid was forced open too far, or was it forced open after seizing shut? For example, imagine you have a dented silver pot where the dent was a trauma from the outside. Logic dictates that it needs to be pushed back out from the inside – what tools and techniques can you use for this?

Has the object been repaired before? If so, what materials and techniques were used? Does any previous work affect how the repair you are about to do should be carried out? All of these thoughts need to be taken into consideration before the first filing, soldering or hammer blow.

SILVERSMITH'S (GUILTY!) SECRET

This really is a secret. I was given a silver pin cushion in the shape of a small bird to repair by a friend while I was in my first year at college. It was split and I needed to solder the side back together. I prepared it, heated it ready to solder and it just collapsed around the joint!

I asked a college tutor where I had gone wrong; had I heated it too much? I was told that someone else had previously tried to solder it with lead solder; my heating (to excess) caused the lead to burn the silver away.

...and another that should perhaps best be kept secret – I heated what I thought was a silver teapot to solder a split between the spout and main body – but it turned out to be made from Britannia metal. The melting temperature of this metal is extremely low and my heating caused the spout to literally melt off and become a pool of molten metal!

Luckily in this case I owned the teapot. I tell you these things so that you can appreciate that we are all capable of making mistakes – it is often how we learn.

WORKING WITH ANTIQUE OR PRECIOUS MATERIALS

I recommend that you practise your skills on scrap metal and items that have little importance. Damaged or broken pieces can be bought in sales, on auction sites and in charity shops for very little. Practise on something that doesn't matter. By doing this you will build up confidence, and subsequently your approach to fixing a cherished piece will be one of assurance and certainty of the outcome.

Once you have confidence in your abilities, and the right tools and techniques, move on to repairing your precious item.

Test pieces
The jug in the background is an irreplaceable antique – and so to minimize the risks, I'm testing out the techniques I intend to use beforehand, on the cheaper jug in the foreground.

CLINIC

At the other end of the financial scale from the cheap jug above, this Nobel prize medal is by far the most valuable item that I have repaired. It is 23.5 Carat gold; almost as fine as is possible to obtain.

I was terribly worried, especially as the client had taken it to some top jewellery shops in London, and they would not accept the repair. The medal was very badly damaged and the client was happy if I could do anything to improve it. I spent a while thinking about it and decided that, ultimately, it was just a metal coin; and that if I felt that it had been worth nothing I would have no problem starting to fix it. Once my mind was in a 'can-do' mode, the repair was okay to do.

Sometimes the challenge is more psychological than practical, so don't defeat yourself before you start.

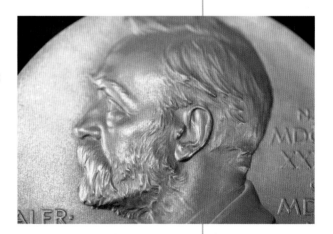

Core skills

The next few pages cover the skills you'll need for silversmithing. Make sure you're comfortable with these core skills before tackling the projects, where you'll see how these skills are applied – and combined – in practice, along with any more specialist techniques.

CUTTING WITH A PIERCING SAW

The main reason to use a piercing saw is that it allows metal to be cut without distortion. If you are using shears or a guillotine to cut metal, the very edge of the metal will be distorted slightly by the pressure, as shown in the illustration to the right. For certain jobs, a little distortion is fine. If, however, you require that the very edge of the metal remains a constant thickness, a saw should be employed.

▶ **THE TOOL** See pages 34–35.

▶ **TYPICAL USE** Re-sizing a ring. When the material is bent around to join the two faces, the edges of the cut faces will not align flush. By cutting with a saw, both sides of the cut remain flat on the bench peg. There is little waste and there is the potential for the offcut to be used for something else, rather than curled up in the scrap container.

PREPARATION

To attach a piercing blade to the frame of the saw, undo the butterfly nuts that hold the clamps, clamp in the end furthest away from you. Run your finger gently up the blade to make sure that it is the correct way around – that is, with the teeth facing downwards. You always cut on the downward stroke with a piercing saw.

With the front of the frame braced against the bench, lean on the handle with the centre of your chest to bend and tension the frame slightly. Tighten the floating end of the blade. Once the pressure from your chest is released, the blade is tensioned in the frame. The blade can be plucked to ascertain tension.

Getting the tension right takes a bit of practice, but it is important: if the blade tension is too loose, it will be hard to saw accurately along a line; if it is too tight, it will break easily and often. A very fine blade may even break as you release the pressure from your chest, a sure-fire (and annoying!) method of finding out it was too tense.

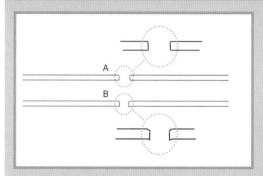

Clean cut and distortion

This diagram shows cross-sections of metal cut with a piercing saw (A) and with a guillotine (B). Compare the clean cut of the piercing saw with the distorted edge resulting from the guillotine.

SECRETS OF THE PIERCING SAW

- *Once your eyesight is as bad as mine, you can check that the blade is inserted the right way round (that is, cutting on the down stroke) by very gently rubbing your finger up the front edge of the blade: you should feel friction. This means the blade is inserted correctly.*

- *Lubrication can be used to prolong the life of the blade. Wax, soap, petroleum jelly, or proprietary cutting lubricant can all be adopted.*

TECHNIQUE

When using a piercing saw, it is important to let the weight of the frame do the cutting, if you start to 'force' the blade, it will inevitably snap.

- Start with your body quite low at the bench: it's the most comfortable position.

- Set the blade tipped forwards at a 45° angle to the material to get the saw going. This offers the teeth a greater surface area of metal to get started on and so the saw will cut the material more easily.

- As you continue to cut, slowly and gradually stand the saw up more vertically until it is perpendicular to the metal.

- If you need to turn a corner, keep the blade moving at all times: it may pinch if you stop moving, then break as you start again.

Start cutting at an oblique angle.

Stand the saw up once the saw has started to cut.

FILING

All types of filing involve rubbing a file over a surface to smooth it out or shape it. More often than not a fine file is used for silversmithing, as a coarse file means more work and potentially more damage – all file marks will eventually need to be reduced to wet and dry marks, getting progressively finer until the object can be polished.

▶ **THE TOOL** See pages 38–39. The right file needs to be used in the right circumstance, hence a good selection is necessary.

▶ **TYPICAL USE** Removing engravings; smoothing areas prior to polishing.

PREPARATION AND TECHNIQUE

When filing, different methods need to be adopted. Generally, the file should be pressed down just enough to make it cut. If you press down too hard, you have less control and could slip, damaging the surface or simply making more work for yourself. Here are some tips:

- Press down on the forward stroke, releasing pressure and lifting off the metal when withdrawing the file. This will help to stop the file clogging.

- If the file becomes clogged, it can put nasty marks on the metal – see below for how to clean it.

- Keep the file flat on the job, if you roll the file onto its edge it can cut in and cause damage.

- Clamp the work and file with two hands wherever possible – one hand holding the handle, the other supporting the front of the file.

- File straight or on a slight diagonal.

REMOVING FILE MARKS

After filing, the surface will have a distinctive texture, which will need to be removed.

Wet and dry paper The most common way of removing the marks left after filing is to use progressive grades of wet and dry paper, wrapped or stuck to a flat surface such as a wooden board. You can make your own, or use emery boards or sticks for this purpose.

Water of Ayr stone An alternative way to level the surface of filed material, Water of Ayr stones can only be used wet. To use one, place the object in a bowl or plastic tray with a little clean water. Pressing down firmly, rub the stone over the hammer facets or file marks on a surface. The stone will gently abrade the high spots. If you pause at this point, the low spots will be clearly visible as a different shade or texture as the cutting face of the stone has not yet reached them. Keep working until the metal is uniform, at which point the surface is levelled off, smooth and ready for polishing.

CLEANING A CLOGGED FILE

I have a theory that a hard steel file brush may blunt a file, so I recommend instead using the edge of a piece of sheet brass or copper to clean or clear a clogged file.

Running the sheet of brass/copper sideways across the 'grain' of the file will soon creates grooves in the sheet. These then start to clear the teeth.

Cleaning a file with a scrap piece of brass – you can see where the clogging has been removed, and where it remains.

Draw filing

Using two hands, the file is 'drawn' along the surface to be filed in a level motion.

Filing an edge

Care must be taken to keep the file flat to the edge. If you don't keep the file on the correct plane, you will round the edge.

Filing top edge with aid of a sand bag

The sandbag provides support and the leather provides some resistance, helping to keep the object firm as filing takes place.

Needle filing fine detail

If you use the correct profile of needle file, even the tiniest detail can be filed.

SECRETS OF FILING

- Never file lead with a good silver file: the lead may contaminate the next piece of silver.
- Before you begin, put masking tape on areas likely to be damaged by catching with the file, to help protect them.
- When a file is worn, keep it as a lead or soft solder file.
- Softer metals can clog a file quite easily.

SOLDERING

Soldering joins metals together by melting solder around the place where they meet. As it cools, if fixes the pieces together. The soldering/heating area needs to be large and well ventilated. The walls should be fireproof plasterboard, brick or stone and the hearth area designed to be safe.

▶ **THE TOOLS** See pages 40–41.

▶ **TYPICAL USE** Permanently connecting metals.

PREPARATION

The most important advice is to know how solder behaves. Solder does not like a dirty surface, nor will it bridge a large gap. Make sure that the joints are surgically clean and that the joint faces are close together. There is no cheating this: if you push your luck, the solder joint won't work.

- When you need to join large areas, you can gradually feed a stick of solder into the area as you work. More often, however, pallions – small pieces of solder cut from the stick – are a better approach.

- More control can be obtained by adding pallions to the joint after adding the flux (see opposite). This method means less cleaning up and filing of excess solder than stick feeding. You can also see when the solder is about to flow as it 'balls up' from its rectangular pallion shape, just before it is about to flow.

- When repairing an area near a previously soldered joint, consider what grade of solder the previous craftsman used. Soldering a new knuckle on a hinge, for example, could cause the hinge bearer to fall off the item when the old solder is heated. Old joints need to be secured with binding wire or supported so they do not come apart.

SECRETS OF SOLDERING

- *I always use silver solder for repairing silver except if the object has previously been repaired with soft solder (as heating it to the temperatures needed for silver soldering will damage the soft solder), or if the item itself would be damaged by heating it to the higher temperatures required.*
- *If I am to use a soft solder, then I favour Staybrite, a tin/silver alloy soft solder, and the flux that comes with it, Stayclean. I find it is usually better to use pallions.*
- *You will not be able to see that the silver has turned red hot (indicating that it is about to melt) in bright daylight, so it is advisable to heat silver in a darkened room. See page 67 for more on heating silver.*
- *Warm the flux slightly with your soldering torch until the water boils away before adding pallions of solder. The violent action of the boiling can eject delicately placed pallions right off the job.*
- *If you suspect a soft solder has been used in a previous repair, never heat silver more than a few hundred degrees centigrade or it will dissolve – see soft solder opposite.*

FLUX

All solder joints require flux prior to heating: solder will not flow and therefore join the metals if flux is not used. It also keeps the joint clean and free from oxidization during heating.

Different metals require different types of flux. Some types of flux come in dropper bottles to allow you to apply it directly, or you can paint the appropriate flux onto the joint with a soft watercolour brush.

Silver soldering The most common flux for silver soldering is borax (see page 41). The brand 'Easy Flow' is a white powder, mixed with water for use with silver solder.

Gold and silver soldering 'Auflux', a yellow/green liquid, is a good product.

Soft soldering Soft solder requires different fluxes. 'Bakers Fluid', 'Stay Clean' and 'LA-CO' are among the many options available.

Tallow This is a flux used for stained glass work.

SOLDERS

There are two distinct types of solder: hard and soft. 'Hard' is an alloy of silver or gold and requires temperatures near the melting points of these metals to melt and flow. 'Soft' solder melts and flows at much lower temperatures. The sort of solder you need will depend on the particular repair you are effecting. Wherever possible, use hard solder; soft solders are the last resort. Only hard solder can be used for items intended to be hallmarked.

Hard silver solder This makes the best repairs in silver, as it is strong. However, the melting temperatures of silver solders are quite close to silver's melting point. Silver solder comes in different grades, from 'Extra Easy' to 'Enamelling', and particular care must be taken when working on fine items, or whenever you are using 'Hard' or enamelling solder, as it is quite easy to melt (damage) sterling silver when using these.

Silver solder type	Melting range
Enamelling	730–800°C (1346–1472°F)
Hard	745–780°C (1373–1436°F)
Medium	720–725°C (1328–1337°F)
Extra Easy	655–710°C (1211–1310°F)

Hard gold solder Gold solders are available in yellow, red, green and white, depending on the colour of gold that is being soldered. Like silver solder, these are also available in different types, ranging from Easy to Hard.

Gold solder type	Melting range
High-carat, Hard	790–830°C (1454–1526°F)
Low-carat, Hard	755–795°C (1391–1463°F)
High-carat, Easy	700–715°C (1292–1319°F)
Low-carat, Easy	650–720°C (1202–1328°F)

Soft solder There are many soft solders. Usually an alloy of tin and other metals, the lower melting temperatures of soft solders can make some repairs easier. They are produced for electrical and electronic soldering, plumbing, stained glass windows and many other applications where an excess of heat should be avoided, most contain a mix of lead and tin.

- The use of soft solder is not permitted for hallmarking purposes.

- Some solders, typically ones used for electrical work, have a flux core.

- There are lead-free alloys, low melting temperature alloys, even solders that melt as low as 70°C (158°F), so boiling water would break the joint.

- Unknown white metals are best repaired carefully with very low melting point soft solders.

- If I am soft soldering silver, I always use a tin/silver solder, such as Staybrite.

Strips of solder, showing the different widths in which it is available. Pallions are tiny pieces cut from these strips.

Sitting on firebricks on a kiln shelf, here are the two pieces of metal to be joined.

TECHNIQUE

Here I'll show you how to solder together two pieces of metal. Remember: cleanliness and a good fit are vital. It will not flow if the parts to be connected are dirty, and can only connect areas that are physically close.

- Place the larger piece on a kiln shelf, on top of fire bricks.

- Use wet and dry paper to key the surface with slight texture where you want the join.

- Use reverse action tweezers to hold the other piece firmly in place.

- Once these parameters are achieved, add flux to the joint. Different fluxes are used depending on whether you require a silver soldered joint or a soft solder joint, but the principles are the same.

- Take the stick of soldier close to the join and use side cutters to trim a small pallion off, then push it into place using tweezers.

- Use a torch to heat the object, observing the temperature. When the correct temperature is reached, the solder will flow into the joint.

- Continue adding pallions and heating them until you reach the end of the area you want to secure.

Using wet and dry paper to key the surface.

The keyed surface.

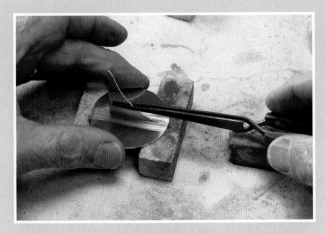

Holding the piece to be joined firmly in place.

Applying flux where the two pieces join.

Trimming a pallion off the stick of solder.

The pallion should be placed as close as possible to where the two pieces of metal meet.

Heating the pallion until it flows into the joint.

The completed soldering.

HAMMERING

Never use your silversmithing hammers for DIY: you will mark the faces. If the hammer has grind marks or pitting in its face, these will transfer to your work: a polished hammer leaves a polished mark, a pitted hammer will impart pitted marks... for each and every blow.

▶ **THE TOOL** See pages 31–33.

▶ **TYPICAL USE** Removing dents, straightening or smoothing surfaces.

PREPARATION

Hammers are versatile tools, but make sure you're using the right one for a particular job.

TECHNIQUE: REPAIRING DENTS

The highly reflective, polished surface of silver (and other metal, for that matter) is amazing at highlighting any flaws. Even small dents will stand out as malformations in the metal. Hammering should be the last resort for these repairs. If at all possible, try to push out a dent with fingers or a burnisher (see page 46), as this will do less damage to the surface of the metal than hitting it with a hammer.

If you do need to use a hammer, tap the inside of the dent with a curve-faced hammer. This will leave the shiny surface of a silver object with ripples, which will need to be removed with planishing.

TECHNIQUE: PLANISHING

Once the dent is removed, the surface needs to be planished. Planishing is usually done from the outside of the object, with the inside supported on a polished stake of the correct profile.

The aim is to gently tap the surface to create very fine, overlapping hammer marks (facets). This planishing slowly removes each high spot, always overlapping the facets, and leaves the metal almost smooth. The face of the hammer needs to have a 'barely-there' convex profile. The hammer must be hit squarely onto the metal or crescent moon shapes will be seen on the surface where the edge of the hammer has struck it. This crescent moon damage is quite hard to remove.

- Ensure you hold the object firmly over the stake.

- Both the hammer and stake you use should be highly polished in order to leave the silver as smooth as possible. If there is a deep file mark or scratch in the face of a hammer, it will be transferred to your work every time you add a blow.

- Every tap with the hammer should produce a ringing sound. If there is a dull or hollow sound when you hit it, the object is not in the correct position on the stake.

- It is important to have the correct stake supporting the object. The more surface area supporting the object, the easier and better the result.

What's happening?

This sectional view shows the (exaggerated) effect the hammer has on the metal as it strikes – it sends ripples through the surface, which need to be smoothed through planishing.

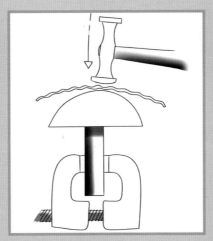

Set-up for planishing

The stake is held in the vice, and the lightly dented bowl being planished is on top of the stake.

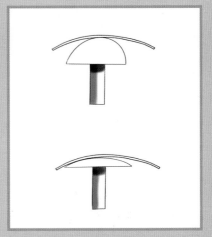

Maximize surface area

A cross-section of incorrect (top) and correct (bottom) stakes for planishing this bowl – you want as much surface area in contact as possible.

TECHNIQUE: SNARLING

A technique for removing dents when you cannot access the inside of an object with a hammer, snarling is a seemingly magical way of applying force to an impossible to reach area using a hammer and snarling iron.

One end of the snarling iron is held firmly in a vice – see right – and the dented object placed over the iron, with the dent located over the middle of the stake on the other end of the iron.

By hitting the bar, the iron bends very slightly down, then bounces back, transferring the energy into the top point of the stake. If it is correctly positioned, it will start to knock the dent up every time the bar is struck. Much practice is needed to do this effectively.

The action of hitting the snarling iron causes it to bounce back up, exerting an upwards force on the dent.

- Knowing how hard to hit is key. It is best to start gently and see how much the dent is rising.

- If you watch the vessel closely, you can see what effect each individual tap is causing.

- Sometimes it is helpful to get someone else to do the hitting; you can then support the item with two hands guiding it to where you need the impacts to be.

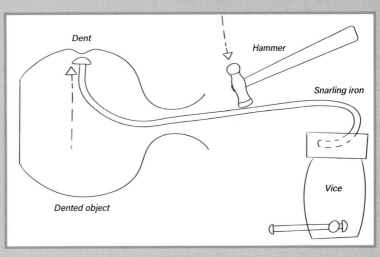

Dent · Hammer · Snarling iron · Vice · Dented object

BURNISHING

A burnisher can push a dent level given the right circumstances.

▶ **THE TOOL** See page 46.

▶ **TYPICAL USE** Removing dents and scratches from items.

PREPARATION

Support the metal needs from behind before attempting burnishing. A leather sandbag is ideal.

TECHNIQUE

Burnishing involves pushing out a dent from the inside, using the polished, hard metal burnishing tool. Simply rub the metal from behind the dent, pressing into the support on the other side.

- The burnisher will slide over the surface of the metal without leaving marks: it can even polish it.

- It is important to choose the correct burnisher.

- The burnisher should be highly polished, to avoid deep scratches and to enable it to glide over the metal.

- Sometimes a planishing hammer can be used as a burnisher.

Identifying the dent

Burnishing is done from behind the dent, with a support on the other side. Here, once the dent is identified, the item is supported on a leather cushion for burnishing.

Using the correct burnisher

in this case I used a flattish, curved burnisher for the middle of the lid and a doming tool where the profile of the lid was more curved.

ANNEALING

Over time metal becomes age hardened. It can also be hardened by working it – that is, hammering. If metal needs to be manipulated, it should be annealed. The process relaxes the molecules in the metal, making it more malleable and therefore more workable.

▶ **THE TOOL** A torch (see page 40) and heatproof surface (see page 42) are needed. Firebricks (also on page 42) are useful, too.

▶ **TYPICAL USE** Making age-hardened metal more workable.

PREPARATION

Place the metal to be annealed on a kiln shelf. It is preferable to raise it slightly off the shelf sitting it on using some bent iron binding wire or iron split pins. By raising it, this allows the metal to heat more quickly. If it is flat against the kiln shelf the heat will 'sink' away into the shelf. Alternatively, small firebricks/blocks can raise the item from the shelf.

TECHNIQUE

Annealing is achieved by heating the metal using a large flame on a propane torch.

Heat the metal as evenly as possible. The whole piece needs to be heated to be red hot – although it is not essential that a large item is all red hot at the same time. Next, you can leave it to cool, or quench it in water – be careful of hot steam and splashes.

Evenly heating pieces of brass, copper and silver sheet. Note that the sheets are raised above the kiln shelf on firebricks.

With the flame removed and the lights off, all the pieces are the same temperature, it can be seen that the silver (on the far right) barely glows. Compare this with the brass (left) and copper (middle).

SILVERSMITH'S SECRET

Enormous care should be taken when annealing silver. The room should be darkened, as really hot silver appears white with only a tiny hint of red. If you see silver as all bright red hot, it has probably melted.

MACHINE POLISHING

The object of polishing is to make the surface as flat and as smooth as possible.

▶ **THE TOOL** See page 44.

▶ **TYPICAL USE** Restoring a mirror finish to a tarnished or newly-repaired item.

PREPARATION

After hammering, manipulating or soldering some filing will be almost certainly necessary. Once the solder or high hammer points are removed by the file, the file marks then need to be removed. By 'filing' with a Water of Ayr stone or progressively fine wet and dry papers on a hard supporting board or stick, the file marks are slowly diminished. You know when it is ready for polishing because the metal is still dull, but feels very smooth to the touch and you cannot see any lines from the file.

Even after the surface has been smoothed with these tools, scratches need to be polished out. The item to be polished should either have a Water of Ayr stone or at least a 1500 grit wet and dry finish. Any coarse sanding or filing lines remaining will probably not polish out and may 'drag' thereby becoming more pronounced.

• Before you begin, ensure you have an extractor underneath the machine, good lighting and, if working on smaller items, a guard.

Unpolished surface
Tarnished, dull and with visible scratches, this surface will need to be prepared with wet and dry paper or a Water of Ayr stone before machine polishing.

Polished surface
If a piece has been repaired and finished correctly, after machine polishing, the surface will have a mirror-like finish, reflective and with no scratches.

TECHNIQUE

Machine polishing can done be with a bench mounted motor or a pendant motor: the same principles apply. A pendant motor gives more control for polishing intricate items, while a bench polishing motor is better for larger pieces – that's what we'll show here.

The polishing is done in stages: firstly with mops loaded with Tripoli compound, then secondly with rouge. Tripoli compound removes the microscopic scratches and starts to give the metal its lustre. Although the metal appears shiny at this point, some very fine scratches remain – the finer rouge polishing process will remove these, leaving a high polish.

- The compounds are introduced to their respective polishing mops while they are rotating.

- A typical bench polishing motor should rotate just under 3000rpm and be 1 or 2hp – and thus safety is important when machine polishing.

- The item should always be directed towards the polishing mop below the centre line. The 'cutting' face of the mop will then be moving away or past the piece, in this way it avoids grabbing it.

- If an edge is addressed to the mop above the centre line, it is likely to be torn from your grip and unceremoniously smashed on the workshop floor – and possibly cause you injury. Always have the mop cutting away from an edge, as shown in the illustration.

Machine polishing safety

The piece is being addressed to the mop below the centre line. Note that the guard has been removed for photography.

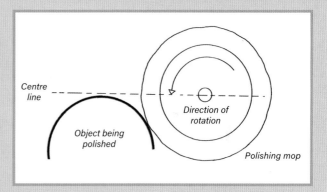

Never address a mop above the centre line or with a sharp edge, as this is likely to catch.

APPLYING COMPOUND

Whether Tripoli compound or rouge, the mop must be loaded with compound prior to polishing. This is done by presenting the compound block to the mop as shown to the right.

Note that, as with anything you present to the mop, it is held below the centre line. Spin the mop until the compound is loaded.

Spinning the mop to apply Tripoli compound.

EXAMPLE OF POLISHING

Having read through the notes on the previous pages, here you can see the stages of bringing a heavily-oxidized copper watering can up to the mirror finish shown to the right.

Addressing the job to the mop

The mop has been loaded with Tripoli compound, and the watering can is brought up to the mop below the centre line.

First polish

You can see the effects of the Tripoli compound gently abrading away the surface dirt and oxidation.

Awkward areas

Swap to a smaller brush mop for difficult-to-reach areas like this.

Final polish

Once you've worked over the whole watering can with the Tripoli-loaded mop, swap to a softer swansdown mop loaded with rouge for the final polish.

TRUING AND LEVELLING

Any piece that stands tall and straight deserves to be level and true. Truing and levelling are techniques that properly shape or align an object; and are important when a piece is damaged.

▶ **THE TOOL** See page 42. Truing is easiest with a potter's decoration wheel. Levelling involves using a engineer's cast iron surface plate and a surface gauge. An engineer's square can also help.

▶ **TYPICAL USE** Ensuring symmetry.

TECHNIQUE: TRUING

Trueness can be measured laboriously or it can simply be placed in the middle of a turntable and spun around gently; any slight wobble becomes clearly visible.

By carefully watching it wobble, we can ascertain how out of true it is. Adjustments can be made and it can then be re-checked.

TECHNIQUE: LEVELLING

If the item has a base, put it on the engineer's plate, making sure that it sits flat. If it rocks, it is not level and needs to be manipulated back into true. Most materials in this book are soft enough to do this by hand, judging by eye as you work. The key is to have an absolutely flat surface – the plate – to ensure accuracy.

The process is similar if the item has feet. Put it on a level plate, and make sure that all of the feet are touching the plate. If not, adjust the offending foot (or feet) as necessary.

This white metal pot had a bent base and could be levelled by hand using thumb pressure only, due to the softness and malleability of the material.

BRUSH PLATING

If the item is not solid silver or gold but looks like it is, it is likely base metal covered – that is, 'plated' – with a thin layer of the previous metal. Any repair made to a silver- or gold-plated item will almost certainly damage or remove the surface plating, which is only a very thin coating.

Small amounts of damage to a plated surface is repairable: the item can be re-plated using a DC power supply and the correct metal salts, after which it will look as it was intended.

▶ **THE TOOL** See page 48.

▶ **TYPICAL USE** Restoring a silver or gold finish to a damaged base metal item.

Using two electrodes, brush plating seems almost magical. A soft cotton swab on the end of a positively-charged electrode 'wand' is soaked with silver salt solution. The other electrode (negatively-charged) is attached to the item you want to plate. When you touch the wand to the item, you close the circuit and the silver molecules in the solution are attracted and fixed to the item. The longer that you wipe the wand, the more microns of silver are deposited, at the rate of around 1 micron thickness per minute. A micron is 1/1000 of a millimetre. It is necessary to try to put on around 30 microns to achieve a good durable surface.

Silver brush plating using a power supply and silver salts.

PREPARATION AND TECHNIQUE

You will need a DC power supply with an adjustable voltage and amperage. Refer to the manufacturer's settings for each type of plating and change it to the correct settings.

- Place the object in a non-conductive dish. A Pyrex dish is ideal, strong and easy to clean. It must never go back into the kitchen as the chemicals may be harmful. Ensure the object is clean and free from dust, dirt and grease.

- Connect the negative cable to any part of the item to be repaired.

- Attach the wand to the positive cable, and soak the swab in silver (or gold, as appropriate) salt solution.

- Bring the soaked cotton swab to the surface of the repaired item and gently begin to brush, keeping the swab in contact throughout.

- Very soon the item will take on its correct colour. The longer that you continue to brush, the thicker the plating.

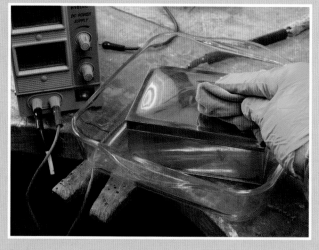

Set up

The piece to be plated in a glass bowl. I like to use a glass dish so that I can see what is going on. The negative metal end of the circuit is simply held onto the bottom of the object (to avoid scratching in a visible place). I hold it in position with my nitrile gloved left thumb.

The solution being added to the positively-charged wand.

The wand being applied to the surface, completing the circuit.

Silver-plating in action – you can see the difference between the re-plated side on the right, and the original surface on the left.

You can continue building up the surface until you are satisfied.

SECRETS OF SILVER PLATING

- *Plating is extremely thin. Silver will attach at less than a micron per minute of brushing.*
- *The process is slow – even a minimal coating of 20 microns will take around twenty minutes for a relatively small area – but you can confirm that it is working by looking at the ampage figure on the power supply – this will change as the connection is made.*

- *Brush plating is only really suitable for small repairs. If you have a large area to plate (or don't want to invest in silver-plating equipment), I recommend finding a commercial plating company. Commercial platers use large silver cyanide tanks in which the whole item is submerged and the electrical process works in a similar way. This is a better and more durable way of plating, but the chemicals are quite hazardous for home use.*

PROJECTS

The following projects are a sample of the type of work that arrives at my workshop daily – a mix of valuable antiques and monetarily worthless but sentimentally priceless objects. Their value has little influence on how I treat them: all are very important to their owner in some way. I have selected these items because they allow me to show you how to fix a range of problems such as removing dents, fixing broken sections, or replacing worn findings. In short, they are representative of the sort of issues that you'll commonly want to fix.

I have aimed for a cross-section of pieces that allow me to showcase as many different skills as I could fit into this volume. Although it's unlikely you'll have exactly the same object, you'll find similar items which are in need of the same sort of repair. For example, the skills you learn in the project on removing engravings could be transferred to, say, jewellery. Another transferrable skill – fixing a wooden handle – will enable you to repair the leg of a wooden animal in a carved Noah's ark set. So rest assured you don't need to find a particular sugar caster or chocolate pot to get going!

You may be coming into your workspace with different aims. You may be a keen repairer with a few tools and just one or two sentimental pieces to fix, or you may wish to buy broken and damaged objects cheaply, 'do them up' and sell them for a profit. The repairs that I teach you here will enable both. Sometimes objects will have several issues: a dent, an inscription and a broken hinge – quite a shopping list. All those problems can be addressed one by one by working your way through my lessons – or if you're feeling more confident, you can dip in and out as necessary and get lots of useful tips.

▶ **ITEM** A silver-plated, Edwardian, sugar caster made by Mappin & Webb Ltd.

▶ **AIM** To remove an unwanted, engraved inscription.

▶ **DIFFICULTY OF REPAIR** Medium.

When a piece has an engraved monogram or message, this can reduce its value on the open market and make it completely undesirable to collectors. Of course, this can be a good thing for someone with the skills to remove the text, perhaps with a view to re-selling.

Removing engraving from jewellery, for example, is often quite handy, as you can give a second-hand identity bracelet a new life as a polished and usable or sellable item. Most items that have engraving should be suitable for these removing techniques. If the piece is solid silver, it makes your life a whole lot easier as you do not need to re-silver plate after polishing. The main thing that you need to look out for is metal that is too thin. If the metal is already thin, filing the engraving might remove half its thickness – and it will become weak and could easily break.

Before

YOU WILL NEED

- Dixième gauge, or other tool to measure thickness
- Crossing needle file, crossing file, file brush
- Wooden battens
- Wet and dry paper
- Double-sided tape
- Polishing tools: pendant motor with flexible shaft, mops and compounds
- Silver-plating kit: power supply, cables, wand, silver anode, pad and silver-plating solution
- Silver polish, soft cloth

The finished repair

Detail of the unwanted engraved inscription.

ASSESSING THE PROBLEM

The first thing to do is to check whether removing the engraving is practical. If the item is too thin or the engraving to deep, removing it can make the object weak or structurally compromised. The thickness of the item should therefore be measured using callipers or a digital thickness gauge before doing anything.

The wall thickness on this caster measures 1.1mm (around 1/32in), which is quite heavyweight and makes it a good candidate for removing the inscription.

The other challenge here is that the piece is silver-plated, rather than solid silver. As a result, we also have to factor in re-plating after polishing.

Measuring thickness

A simple but effective tool for measuring thickness, the dixième gauge is a calliper that indicates the dimension between its fingers on the numbered scale on the opposite side.

By opening the spring-loaded fingers and letting them compress on a piece, the thickness is then shown.

SECRETS OF CHECKING THICKNESS

If you're unable to measure a piece for whatever reason – perhaps you've spotted it in a second-hand shop or thrift store and don't have your tools on you – you can still get a feel for a piece simply by holding it and inspecting it to get a sense of its gauge. This of course takes a bit of practice, but the following tips are good starting points for helping to assess whether the item is thick enough to stand an unwanted engraving being removed:

Depth of the engraving *Look at the depth of the engraving should help you to make an evaluation of whether the item is suitable for engraving removal. Some engraving, including bright-cut, is so deep – sometimes more than half the thickness of the construction material – that removal would render the piece so thin that it would become unusable.*

Type of object *Boxes are often made from quite light gauge metal and strengthened by lining with wood. Removing an engraving from these can be quite risky, leaving the metal too thin and weak.*

Filled items *Candlesticks or silver hand mirrors and brushes are commonly filled, which means they are made from very thin metal that is formed and filled with a solid filler such as pitch or plaster to give strength and weight. Such items are not suitable for the processes described here, as the silver surface is too thin.*

Visible outdent *Sometimes if the backing is removed from a box or the pitch from a mirror, the outdent of the engraving can be seen on the reverse of the metal. In these instances, removal should be avoided, because this indicates that the metal is dangerously thin and in danger of falling apart.*

Wall thickness

The silver here is relatively thick. As an observation, it feels heavy for its size, a good indicator – though not a guarantee – that this technique will be suitable.

Removing the engraving with the file. The face of the file remains parallel to the curve of the item, as shown.

Wet and dry paper wrapped around a 'crossing' file and held in place, ready to be used to remove the file marks.

REMOVING THE ENGRAVING

The curved convex surface of this sugar caster is an ideal surface from which to remove the engraving. This is because it is relatively easy to file and polish due to the raised, exposed surface – imagine filing a spoon bowl: the outside or bottom would be easy to file whereas the inside of the bowl would be very hard to file.

The result we want is a smooth finish, so everything we do here hangs around the idea of avoiding adding new marks while we remove the unwanted engraving.

While working, it is important to make sure that the file does not clog with metal, as this will also mark the metal. The file can be cleaned with a bespoke file brush (see page 50) or with a piece of brass or silver (see page 58).

- With a fine-cut 'crossing' needle file, and keeping the file face flat, file along the concave surface of the caster. Be careful not to roll the file on its edge, as this will dig in and make deep marks.

- Start to remove the engraving. It is important to work evenly over the whole area and not start on one letter before the next. Working on the complete engraving at the same time avoids making obvious flat areas or marks that would result in ripples in the final finish.

- Once the engraving has been filed away, the file marks need to be removed. This is done using 240 grade wet and dry abrasive paper, rolled around a larger crossing file. You can simply hold the abrasive paper in place.

- File in exactly the same way as with the needle file, keeping the cutting face of the abrasive paper flat. Any undulations or ripples in the metal should be removed as well as the original file marks.

- When the marks have been removed with the 240 grade wet and dry paper, progress to 400, 800, then 1200 grades in turn. Each time, look to see that the marks from the previous grade are removed and, most importantly, that the file marks are eliminated.

Removing file marks with wet and dry paper – again, the tool is kept at the same angle throughout the process.

CLINIC: REMOVING AN ENGRAVING FROM A FLAT-TOPPED BOX

To remove an engraving from something flat, an even amount of metal has to be removed over the whole surface. Otherwise a dip will be formed as you work around the engraved area, and this anomaly will draw the eye once the piece is re-polished.

The important thing is that you keep as much of the file's working face flat to the surface as you work. The process of 'filing' is exactly the same as described for the curved file, except that you keep the cutting face flat. Working in this way, any undulations or ripples in the metal across the whole surface will be removed, rather than just in one particular area.

When removing the file marks from an item with a flat face, you can use shop-bought emery boards – or make your own wet and dry boards, as described to the right.

Home-made wet and dry boards

Save money by attaching wet and dry paper to a flat wood baton, roughly 20 × 8 × 180mm (¾ × ¼ × 7in). These dimensions are not critical, as long as the cutting face is flat. The wet and dry paper is stuck to the wood using carpet layer's double-sided tape.

This box had an unwanted engraving right in the centre of the flat lid.

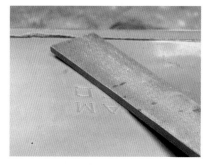

I used a flat file to remove an even amount of material from across as much of the flat surface as possible, rather than focussing more tightly on the engraving itself.

Once the engraving had gone, I used a flat wet and dry board to remove the file marks.

POLISHING

At this stage the base metal can be clearly seen where the silver plate has been filed and sanded. Now the file marks are removed and the progressively finer grades of wet and dry paper have been used, it is time to polish the fine abrasive paper marks from the surface.

A traditional rotating polishing machine can be used for this task, using small mops. In this particular case, as the item is so small, I've opted instead to use a pendant motor with a flexible shaft for the polishing stage.

- Start polishing the surface using Tripoli compound on a cotton mop, following the technique on page 69.
- Pause to check the surface every so often. Once happy that all of the wet and dry marks are removed, you can move on to the final polish.
- Create the finishing lustre using rouge compound on a swansdown or fine cotton mop.

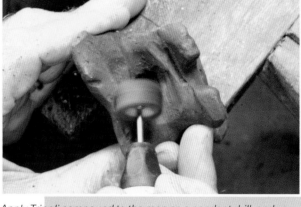

Apply Tripoli compound to the mop on a pendant drill, and you are ready for polishing.

SECRETS OF MACHINE POLISHING

Built through experience, the following list will give you a great path to follow whenever you are machine polishing:

- *Always smooth the metal correctly, making sure ripples are removed.*
- *If you cut corners, it will show in the final polish.*
- *Coarse abrasion marks will not polish out. Before machine polishing, any coarse marks from filing need to be reduced by using finer and finer wet and dry paper until it is ready to polish.*
- *First polish: Tripoli on a cotton mop.*
- *Final polish: rouge on a swansdown mop.*
- *Never get Tripoli on your rouge mop.*
- *Always follow safety precautions using a polishing machine.*

Polishing with Tripoli compound on a cotton mop.

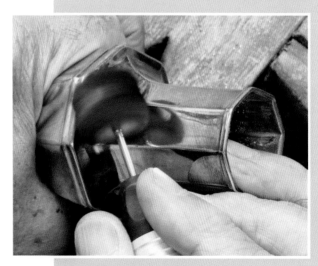

Final machine polishing, rouge on a swansdown mop.

At this stage you can clearly see the base metal, which is nickel.

SILVER PLATING

After filing and polishing, the base metal where the work has taken place will stand out clearly, and this needs to be covered to match the rest of the undamaged silver-plated surface. Clean the metal with pre-plating cleaner using a very soft cloth before you start the silver-plating process.

- Place the item in a waterproof dish, switch the power supply on and add some silver-plating solution to the brush/pad.
- Hold the negative terminal on the inside of the item. Don't use crocodile clips as they can scratch.
- Brush the positive wand over the area to be plated. It is important to keep the wand moving, or you risk the plating 'burning', or going dark.
- A layer of around one micron per minute is added by continual brushing. I usually aim for a layer of around two microns – this will keep the piece silver for many years if it is polished correctly.

Power supply and cables, ready to attach to the sugar caster and wand.

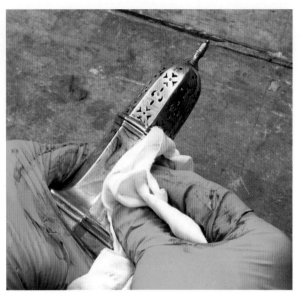

Final polishing by hand.

FINISHING

Once the repair is complete and the area has been machine polished and re-plated, a final gentle hand polish will complete the repair. Do this with a very soft cloth and a quality silver polish.

SECRETS OF REMOVING ENGRAVINGS

Whatever the item, there's a simple checklist to follow when removing an engraving from silver:

- *Ensure the item is indeed solid silver by checking for the presence of a hallmark.*
- *Check that the silver has enough gauge (thickness) to remove the engraving without excessively weakening the structure.*
- *File the area carefully.*
- *Smooth with wet and dry paper.*
- *Polish using Tripoli and rouge and the correct mops.*

The finished repair can be seen on page 77.

▶ **ITEM** 1 oz. sterling silver ingot pendant. London, 1977, maker unknown.

▶ **AIM** To replace worn jump ring.

▶ **DIFFICULTY OF REPAIR** Easy.

Jump rings are small hoops typically used to attach and secure jewellery. You can buy them ready-made, but if you have the skills to make your own from wire, you can match the colour and size you want much more easily. That's what we'll learn in this project, and it's a skill that'll help you repair everything from car keyrings to precious jewellery, like this personal piece.

Before

YOU WILL NEED

- Side cutters
- Vernier gauge
- Piercing saw
- Round-nose pliers
- Spring tweezers
- Tweezers

- Solder, flux small brush
- Tungsten probe
- Pendant drill, polishing mops
- Small soldering torch
- Silver wire
- Piercing saw

The finished repair

ASSESSING THE CHALLENGE

It's immediately obvious that this ingot has been well-loved and worn constantly – in fact, I've had it for over forty years. Through wear and tear, the jump ring that attached the ingot to a chain is nearly worn though – and it wouldn't take much at this point for it to slip free and disappear unnoticed.

It is important to me that it is never lost, so the repair is crucial. By simply replacing the jump ring, future loss due to breakage will be avoided.

Worn finding

You can see clearly how worn through the original jump ring is.

Hallmark

The hallmark on this silver ingot is itself integral to the design, and is clear and easy to read. The sponsor's mark is tiny, so an enlarged detail is shown above.

The lion's head indicates that it was assayed in London, the lack of a crown showing it's a relatively modern piece, while the whole lion facing left states it to be sterling silver.

The 'C' design indicates it was assayed in 1977, and this is borne out by the head of Queen Elizabeth II below the date mark – a commemorative mark to celebrate the occasion of her 25th Jubilee.

Cutting off the old jump ring.

REPLACING THE JUMP RING

The first job is simply to cut the old jump ring off. Save the old metal in the scrap container as it can be melted down and used again.

After this we'll construct and attach a brand new jump ring.

- Use a pair of side cutters to clip away the worn old jump ring.
- Once the old ring is removed, measure its diameter using the vernier gauge.
- Find a suitable round bar of the same inner diameter as the original ring. The new ring will be formed around this. In this case, the top of a scriber was the perfect size.
- Wrap silver wire of a suitable gauge – I used 1mm diameter – around the rod several times, to form neat circles.

Forming the new jump rings by wrapping wire around a rod.

SECRETS OF JUMP RINGS

- *Using the correct wire gauge is important when making your own jump rings – and the best guide to this is simple observation. You will know simply by looking at a jump ring that you have made whether the gauge is in scale with the diameter of the ring.*
- *If you saw the ring carefully, it will just squeeze shut, ready to be soldered shut.*

- Remove this silver 'spring' from the forming bar, then cut across the spring, as shown left. This will form a number of small rings.
- Open up each little ring using either a piercing saw or a fine-toothed parting saw. This way a few spares can be made and kept reserved in a suitable container.
- Select one ring and slip it through the eye at the top of the ingot.
- Using two pairs of pliers, grip the ring on either side of the opening.
- Gently close the ring so that the two ends are touching each other, and the ring forms a perfect circle.

Cutting the spiral into separate jump rings takes just a single cut.

Using pliers to grip both ends of the wire.

Closing the ends of the ring.

SOLDERING

To make the join permanent, and remove the risk of the jump ring opening up, we now solder the join.

- Put some flux onto the joint using a small paintbrush. I used Auflux.

- Balance the ring in the air in preparation for soldering.

- Cut some very small pallions of easy silver solder, using sharp side cutters.

Applying flux to the join.

CLINIC: CREATING GOLD JUMP RINGS

Gold jump rings can be made in a similar way to the silver rings described here. The key things to note here are:

- Gold wire can be made from melting scrap gold and 'drawn down' using a draw plate.

- The same flux can be used for both silver and gold.

- Gold jump rings will require the correct coloured gold solder.

- Gold solders are available in various colours, melting temperatures and carat quality.

Cutting pallions. This particular round solder wire has been hammered flat to make it even thinner so that tiny pallions can be made.

SECRETS OF SOLDERING

There are six secrets to successful soldering – follow these closely and you'll get it right every time.

- *Cleanliness.*
- *A good fit.*
- *Use the correct flux.*
- *Use pallions – it is easier to add more solder this way and will save lots of excess solder removal (filing).*
- *Do not overheat.*
- *Heat evenly.*

Placing the solder on the ring where it joins. Note how small the flame is.

- Gently heat the ring with a small gas/oxygen torch (a small propane torch can be used instead) and pick up a pallion using a tungsten probe that has been moistened with flux. The tungsten probe will not melt, nor will the solder stick to it. This makes it an ideal tool.

- Working carefully, use the tungsten probe to manipulate the pallion into place on the break in the wire ring.

- Remove the probe and heat the ring until the solder flows.

Heating the jump ring needs to be done delicately, as the ring needs to remain separate from the ingot: it's the ring alone that needs to be heated.

If you wanted the ring to be soldered directly to the top of the ingot, a larger torch would be required as the whole ingot would need to reach soldering temperature for the solder to flow.

Carefully heating the ring will get the solder to flow across the joint.

CLEANING AND POLISHING

With the ring secured, the area simply needs to be cleaned and polished to make it ready.

- Once the ring (and ingot) have cooled, the solder can be cleaned using a rotary pointed fine rubber grinding wheel in a pendant drill.
- Give it a final polish with Tripoli using a fine brush mop.
- Then use rouge polish using a swansdown mop to finishes off the ring – it should easily last another forty years.
- A chain can then be re-threaded through the ring to finish.

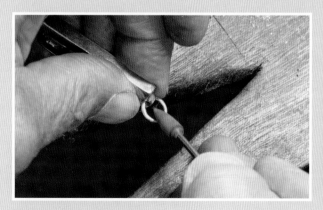

Cleaning solder off the joint.

Tripoli polish on cotton mop.

The finished repair can also be seen on page 84.

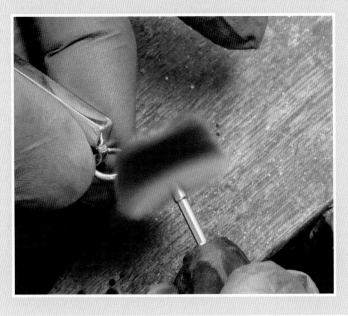

Giving the piece a final polish with rouge compound.

FIXING A WOODEN HANDLE

▶ **ITEM** Chocolate pot, silver-plated with a fruitwood handle, with no maker's marks.

▶ **AIM** To repair the handle, which has broken at the point that it meets the socket on the pot.

▶ **DIFFICULTY OF REPAIR** Medium.

Broken handles where the wood meets the metal are common in this sort of pot. It is possible that this is an early twentieth century copy of an older design. As there is no hallmark or maker's mark on this chocolate pot, perhaps it is a cheaper imitation of a silver piece, intended for the mass market – silver will always have a hallmark, so it's likely that this is silver plate.

The skills you learn here will allow you to repair a range of mixed-material items: salad utensils, old wooden toys, wooden sculptures, candle snuffers and letter openers, as just a few examples.

Before

YOU WILL NEED

- Hammer
- Punch
- Parallel pliers
- Drill and drill bits
- Epoxy adhesive
- Brass wire or stainless steel pins
- Mixing board, mixing stick, old piercing saw blade
- Tape
- Scalpel

- Vernier gauge
- Wire wool
- French polish
- Wax polish
- Cloth
- Felt-tip pen
- Scrap wood
- Clamp

The finished repair

ASSESSING THE CHALLENGE

Wooden handles on silver beverage pots are susceptible to becoming damaged over time, usually at the meeting point between metal and wood. The reason for this is that water creeps into the gap between the tube and the wood when the pots are washed. It then soaks into the wood. Over time and repeated wetting, the wood becomes weak and the joint breaks.

That's likely what has happened here. Sometimes it is necessary to carve a whole new handle. On this occasion, after inspecting the wood, it appears in good condition. However, if the wood was just glued back together, it would break again in a short time, so we need to pin and glue the joint to give it some extra strength.

While we don't need to carve a new handle, the existing handle is also dull and has some spots of white paint on it – a good polish will restore a good-looking finish.

The damage here is quite clean, and the wood remains in good condition.

REMOVING THE HANDLE

The first task is to remove the broken stub from the socket. If this is in good condition, it can be reused. If it is completely rotten, then a new stub needs to be made.

- Getting the correct position to tap can be quite tricky. Using a piece of scrap wood to help support and keep the handle accessible can make positioning the pin easier.
- Using a small centre punch, and carefully supporting the back of the socket, gently tap the pin holding the handle in place.
- Tap the pin until you can grip it with a pair of parallel pliers. Take care not to squeeze the pliers too hard, as you could potentially damage the pin or another will need to be made.

Lining up to tap out the pin. I used a broken burr as a small central punch here.

Tapping the pin with a hammer and centre punch to start to loosen the pin.

SILVERSMITH'S SECRET

If you find that the stub is rotten or damaged beyond repair, it is possible to saw the stub from the handle where it meets the metal socket.
A new stub can be made from the correct size wooden dowel (if it is round) or carved from an offcut.

Using parallel pliers to pull out the pin.

WHAT NEXT?

Once the pin is out the next part can be either easy or tricky. If the stub is moving about in the socket once the pin is removed, with a bit of manipulating using a small probe and pointed pliers, it should come out.

If it doesn't yield, a small hole can be drilled into it and a small self-tapping screw secured into the hole itself. By gripping the screw, twisting and pulling at the same time, it should pull free.

If, in the worst-case scenario, it has been glued in, then it needs to be drilled out carefully, using a small screwdriver to remove the bits. In this case a new stub would need to be made.

- Consulting the notes above and on the previous page, carefully remove the stub of the handle and place it beside the other part (or parts).
- Offer the two parts of the handle together to check the fit.
- If they marry correctly, mix equal parts of epoxy glue on a piece of spare paper and use a coffee stirrer (or similar) to apply it to one surface of the handle.
- Push the pieces together and clamp in position until the glue has cured.
- Clean off any residual glue with a scalpel.

Checking the fit of the broken pieces.

Mixing and applying epoxy adhesive in equal amounts.

Gluing and clamping the handle.

Removing excess glue.

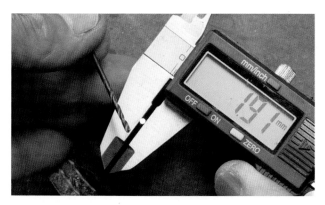

Using a pen to make the marks.

Measuring the pin diameter allows you to select a suitable drill bit.

Drilling the holes for splint pins.

PREPARING TO PIN

The handle should fit back into its socket now. A trial run is recommended. Once you have got it to fit, two holes need to be drilled from the bottom of the stub into the handle itself, to be able to accept pins or splints.

Pinning is a useful way to strengthen a repaired joint. While I used 2mm brass wire for the pins, stainless steel pins can be used, and old discarded pop rivet nails are also handy to use.

- Mark the line on the base of the handle, parallel to the original pin. Then make a mark on either side of the line, each halfway between the centre line and the edge of the circle that makes up the handle stub. Measure this carefully.

- Cut two splint pins from 2mm brass wire. The length of each pin is determined by measuring the stub of the handle, and adding at least 10mm (½in) into the handle beyond the original break.

- Use the vernier gauge to choose a suitable drill bit, then drill the holes at the marks.

SECRETS OF DRILLING

It is possible, if you drill too deeply, to make the drill protrude onto the narrow turned part of the handle. To avoid this, wrap a small piece of masking tape around the drill bit to give a depth guide.

Making a 'depth guide' using tape. Place the pin in line with the tip of the drill bit, then wrap the tape around the bit, in line with the bottom of the pin.

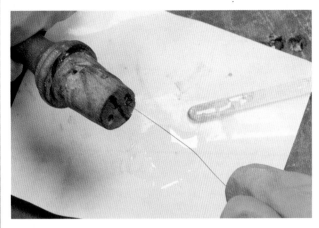

Preparing and applying the glue, as described on page 96.

Tapping the pins into the handle gently.

SECURING THE PIN

- Use a piece of fine wire or similar long, thin item to introduce two-part epoxy glue into the holes. I used an old, broken piercing saw blade because the teeth hold the glue well and the blade is also stiff enough to enable you to get to the bottom of the hole. It is important that the glue is distributed evenly inside the holes.

- Put the pins into their holes and tap in. A satisfying ooze of glue may be seen at the top of the pins, indicating that there is plenty of glue.

- Once the glue has set, file the end so it is flush.

- Measure the locating pin and select a drill the same size. Run the drill though the original hole to clear any adhesive that is blocking it after gluing.

Cross-drilling the original hole to accept the original pin.

CLINIC

An alternative to pinning that may come in useful for this sort of repair is creating a splint, which is shown on page 151. There, a tubular splint does the job of a pin, making the glued joint integral with the two pieces joined.

FINISHING

All that remains is a few finishing touches to restore the pot and handle to their original state, and then the pot can be reassembled.

Note that the pot can be polished at any point once the handle is removed – you might take the opportunity earlier, while you wait for the glue to dry, for example.

- Hand polish the pot with a good-quality silver polish and a soft cloth.
- Before fitting the handle, sand it using a 320 sand paper, then a 600 to remove scratch marks.
- Apply two or three coats of French polish to the handle using a wadded cloth. Use wire wool (Grade 0000) to 'de-nib' between coats, once each has dried.
- Finish the polishing with some wax polish.
- The handle can then be put in position in its socket. Now push firmly, making sure that the holes line up.
- Push the pin back in to finish. The handle should be sitting tight, straight and with no hint of a wobble.

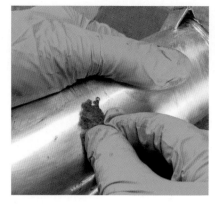
Polishing the pot.

Sanding the handle.

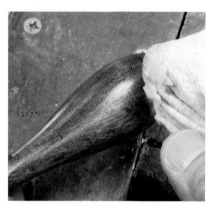
Applying the wax polish.

Securing the handle with the pin.

The finished repair can be seen on page 93.

► **ITEM** Sterling silver cutlery.

► **AIM** To repair and return three items of cutlery to working use.

► **DIFFICULTY OF REPAIR** Easy.

This project is a great introduction to repair; the principles learned are relevant to all utensils and could encompass such pieces as ladles or seafood tools, the list is expansive. I have chosen the three most common pieces of cutlery that we find in our drawers, as these are most used and subjected to wear and tear and – dare I say? – abuse. (I may once have broken a butter knife doing up a screw with it...)

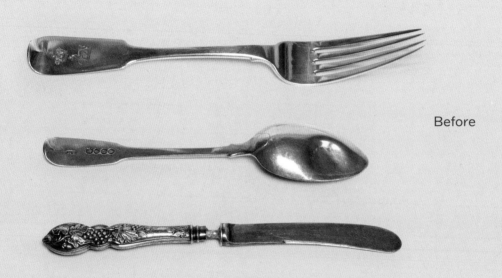

Before

YOU WILL NEED

- Sandbag
- Doming hammer
- Planishing hammer
- Spoon stakes
- Vice
- Small torch or container of boiling water

- Pliers
- Files
- Wet and dry boards
- Polishing machine

The finished repair

ASSESSING THE CHALLENGE

Knives that have hollow handles should never be put into a dishwasher: the heat can make the supporting pitch melt and the blades can become dislodged or even fall out. That's exactly what has happened to the knife in this project.

Spoon
The big dent in the bowl is an obvious problem for this spoon!

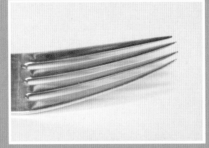

Fork
The tines of this poor piece of flatware have been bent and worn to very sharp points.

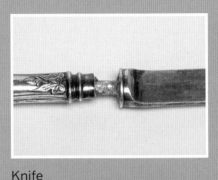

Knife
The knife has been in a dishwasher, melting the supporting material inside the hollow handle and forcing the blade out.

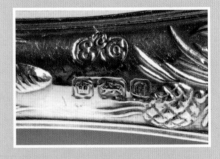

Hallmarks

If it wasn't clear from the varied designs, the hallmarks show that these pieces come from different makers, a range of times, and have been assayed in different places. The spoon (above left), was made by Mary Chawner in 1839, and was assayed in London.

The fork (above centre), dates from 1803, and was likewise assayed in London – note that the assay office mark differs slightly from that of the spoon, as the 'crowned leopard' of the London Assay Office was changed to an 'uncrowned leopard' in 1820. The maker is only recorded as 'IB'.

Both of these items also bear 'duty marks'; portraits of the reigning monarch. This additional mark was introduced in 1784 and abolished in 1890. This explains its absence from the knife (above right), which dates from 1908, as indicated by the lower case blackletter 'q' date mark. It appears to be made by Elkington & Co Ltd, based in Birmingham; although the crown indicates this was assayed in Sheffield.

Both the knife and spoon are sterling silver, as indicated by the 'lion passant' symbol, while the fork is made from Britannia silver.

Knocking the dent back from the inside of the bowl.

DENT REMOVAL AND PLANISHING THE SPOON

This spoon has a large dent in its bowl. This can be knocked back out by supporting the spoon on a leather sand bag.

- Using a doming hammer, gently tap the dent until it is removed.
- The bowl will have marks and ripples after this procedure. To remove these marks, the bowl needs to be planished.
- Put a spoon stake in a vice and place the spoon over this. With a flat, small, highly polished planishing hammer, gently planish (see page 64).
- Once the bowl appears even, a final very gentle planish will soften and blur away the original planishing marks.
- If this has been done correctly, it is just a matter of filing the hammer marks out with wet and dry boards and polishing (see pages 58–59 and 69 for the respective techniques).

The dent has been removed – but note the marks and ripples left by the doming hammer.

SECRETS OF PLANISHING

Just as you aim to hit a tennis ball in the centre of the racquet, not near the frame, planishing has a 'sweet spot'. To identify whether you've got the spot right, listen closely.

The sound of the planishing hammer hitting the spoon should be a clear ringing sound. This means that the spoon is being held correctly on the stake and that the dent will be smoothed out evenly. If the sound is hollow, the dent isn't being smoothed out evenly.

Final planishing.

Removing the planishing marks using a 800 grade wet and dry stick.

RESHAPING AND FILING THE FORK

The tines on the fork are bent and have been polished to very sharp points.

- With flat-nosed, flat-faced (unserrated) pliers gently ease the tines out until they are parallel. It is best to work on the two outside tines first.

- Keep checking until it looks right by eye.

- Once the tines are parallel from the top view, inspect the fork from the end, looking down on the points towards the handle, to make sure the tines line up in that plane too.

- The ends now need to be filed flat and even. Using a flat file, file the points so that they are even. File as little as possible as you do not want the tines to become too short.

- Look at the fork from both faces and see that it looks like a fork, the tines the same length and flat along the top in appearance.

- An optional final stage is to further smooth the tines with a fine abrasive wheel in a pendant drill. Care must be taken to make sure that the abrasive wheel runs 'off', that is, in the direction of the end of the fork. Otherwise the abrasive wheel will grab. This can damage the wheel – and, at the very least, 'grabbing' will make you jump!

The bent tines.

Straightening the tines.

Filing the ends level.

Filing the detail of the tines.

Smoothing the file marks.

Warming the handle.

REFITTING THE KNIFE

The knife blade has fallen part way out after being heated in a dishwasher, and it has set in the wrong position as it cooled. This is an easy repair; a little patience is required. Wear leather gloves to protect you from the heat.

- Gently warm the handle with a small torch to soften the pitch inside the handle. Alternatively, you can place the knife in boiling water for a couple of minutes.
- When the pitch has become molten, push the two parts together and check the alignment of the handle and the blade.
- Leave to cool and clear off any pitch that may have oozed out of the joint. It should just rub off.
- Polish (see page 69).

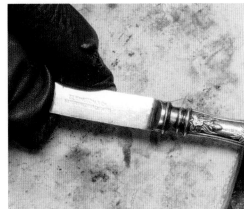

Pushing the two halves together firmly.

Checking that the blade is in correct alignment.

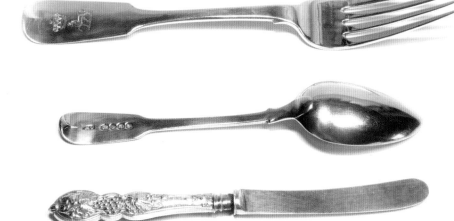

The finished repair can be seen on page 101.

▶ **ITEM** Sterling silver inkwell by Barker Brothers Ltd, Birmingham 1933.

▶ **AIM** To repair the broken hinge.

▶ **DIFFICULTY OF REPAIR** Hard.

The Barker Brothers mass produced utilitarian silverware. They manufactured popular styles of the era. This ink well, with its Art Deco lines and detailing, is no exception.

Any object that has a hinge can be treated this way: card cases, cigarette boxes, tankards, fancy lighters. The only danger is that you have to be able to get the whole of the old pin out or you may end up replacing the whole hinge. This can be quite tricky on some items.

Before

YOU WILL NEED

- Jug, water
- Screwdriver
- Sharp knife
- Masking tape
- Vernier gauge
- Needle files
- Silver chenier
- Silver solder
- Iron binding wire

- Anti-firestain paste (Argotect)
- Flux
- Small paintbrush
- Tweezers
- Potter's kiln shelf or other suitable soldering base
- Soldering torch
- Broach set

- Saw
- Tapered brass pins
- Pendant drill and polishing mops
- Polishing compounds
- Plaster of Paris
- Safety pickle
- Cloth
- Flat graver

The finished repair

ASSESSING THE CHALLENGE

This inkwell has a silver band and a hinged lid that is bonded to the crystal. Silver is often attached to crystal to make either a lid or neck for a stopper. The silver band is a tight fit to the crystal which has had its surface roughed as a 'key' for adhesion. The silver is attached with wet plaster. Once this has set, the silver is secured firmly. It is important to be able to reverse this affixing in case any maintenance is required, as in this example.

If you are very lucky, it is a bearer in the lid that has become damaged and you will not need to remove the bottom part. Nine times out of ten, unfortunately, it is the part attached to the crystal that needs the work.

The repair will require the two missing knuckles to be re-made and soldered in their correct positions. If soldering takes place while still attached to the bottle, it will break the crystal. It therefore needs to be removed for repair.

Before we can do anything with an item like this, it needs to be soaked in warm water for long enough for the plaster to loosen up. This can take several days – so the sooner you start, the better!

Hallmark

Although the maker's mark is slightly worn, the distinctive shield surround of Barker Brothers Silver Ltd remains distinctive. The letters read 'B.B. S.L^D'. Assayed in Birmingham, as shown by the anchor, the lion shows this to be sterling silver, and the capital J date mark shows it to be from 1933.

Unfortunately, the hinge knuckles have broken from the bearer, separating the lid from the inkwell. The knuckles can wear through due to over-use or, more likely, can break off when the hinge has become seized and the lid is forced open. This is quite common if an iron or steel pin has been used, as it can rust and lock the hinge solid in time.

Soaking the inkwell in water.

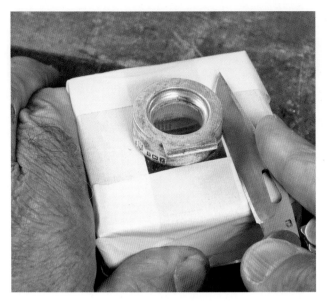

SEPARATING THE PLASTER FROM THE SILVER

Once the inkwell has been in the water for the prescribed time, the silver needs to be removed. In this case, the band was attached with plaster.

- Put some masking tape on the crystal to avoid slipping and scratching it.
- With a fine blade, ease under the edge, rotating the inkwell to perform an even lift of the silver band. If the soaking has been thorough, the band should come free quite easily.
- Once the lid band is free of the crystal, the remaining plaster needs to be removed and cleaned away. You can use any relatively sharp tool for this, but be careful not to damage it.

Gently prising the lid band from the crystal.

Removing the remaining wet plaster using a small flat-headed screwdriver.

SILVERSMITH'S SECRET

If the band doesn't move, it may have been attached with a hide glue or shellac. In either case, gently warm the water (avoiding any thermal shock to the crystal). Once it is between 80°C and 100°C (176°F and 212°F), wearing gloves, try to pull the silver free.

SOLDERING

Any areas that are soldered need to be spotlessly clean for the solder to run properly, so we need to carefully remove the old solder and dirt in preparation for re-soldering.

In this case, as two knuckles have fallen off, the bearer can be filed. If one knuckle had remained in place, it would impede filing. To clean the bearer it would then be necessary to use a pendant drill and small round burr or a round scraper.

- Clean the area where the knuckles came away with a small round needle file.
- The 'U'-shaped channel should be shiny and bright. In this case the base hinge knuckles are missing; so new knuckles need to be made. Measure the diameter of lid knuckle. In this particular case it is 2.43mm.
- Try to obtain some silver chenier of the correct dimensions. The closest was 2.38mm, which is fine for the job.
- Cut two pieces of chenier (knuckles) to the correct length and file the ends using a jointing cutting tool. The tool ensures that the ends of the tube are completely flat and marry up when placed together.

SILVERSMITH'S SECRET:

I made my jointing tool aeons ago at college. Jointing tools are now available with a stop to ensure that all of the knuckles are the right length.

Cleaning the bearers with a fine needle file.

Measuring the diameter of the knuckles.

Confirming the correct diameter chenier – it

Filing the ends flat after cutting in a jointing tool.

The knuckles wired in position.

Applying anti-firestain paste.

- Put the knuckles into their bearer and tie into place using iron wire. This is to stop them moving when the flux inevitably bubbles up as you heat – it can be infuriating to spend time getting pieces in the correct position only to have them shift as they're heated. Once wired, check that they are in the correct place by offering the lid up to the base.

- It is best to coat the silver in a protective barrier to help ease the appearance of firestain (which presents as a red or purple stain) before soldering. Use a flux such as Argotect as the barrier to stop air reaching most of the surface as you heat. This will keep it clean and reduce firestain.

- Flux the joint with borax paste or Auflux using a small paintbrush. Cut two pallions of Easy grade solder and after an initial warming to boil the water from the flux, place them in the middle of the joint. Using gravity to help is always useful as the solder can often fall off if it is 'balanced' precariously.

- Heat gently until the solder first balls up and then flows into the joint. A shiny line can be observed; at this point you know that the solder has flowed correctly.

- Let the part cool down, remove the iron wire, put it in safety pickle solution to remove remaining flux and clean the debris away.

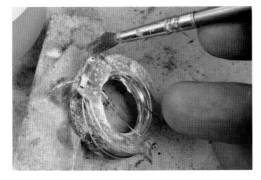

Applying flux to the joint.

Applying the solder pallion.

Keep the flame moving while gently heating the solder.

Place in safety pickle.

Broaching the joint.

REASSEMBLING THE INKWELL

If the soldering has been successful, the two parts can be put together. Looking though the ends of the tube, the passageway should be clear and unobstructed.

- Check that the joint fits. If the parts do not quite line up, look for a ring of excess solder at the ends of the new knuckles. This can be carefully removed with a flat graver. At a right angle to the knuckle, run the graver around the solder joint to remove the excess.

- Next, with the joint held together in the correct position, run a small broach in from one end, twisting between finger and thumb gently applying pressure. The aim of this is to end up with a tapered hole that is in line. Finally insert a tapered brass pin and mark the ends.

- Cut the pin to length and fit.

- Before reassembly, clean the crystal bottle.

- Mix a little plaster of Paris and using it to 'glue' the base back on, any excess can be wiped off with a damp cloth. This needs to be left overnight to dry thoroughly.

Checking the correct length for the pin.

Checking that the pin fits correctly.

Applying the wet plaster to the lid carrier.

Wiping away the excess plaster.

The finished repair can be seen on page 107.

Before

▶ **ITEM** Sterling silver hand mirror by AE Goodby and Son of Birmingham, 1907.

▶ **AIM** Replace figure's nose, remove dents, replace mirror and make new bezel.

▶ **DIFFICULTY OF REPAIR** Hard.

Repairing filled silver – which, as the name suggests, means a thin 'shell' of silver is filled with pitch to give it strength and rigidity – presents some interesting challenges. This mirror offers great opportunity to show how to succeed, as it includes a lot of common problems.

Other items that are similarly 'filled' with pitch include brushes, candlesticks, some silver picture frames and some silver paperweights. In all these case, you will need to melt the pitch as described to remove it before carrying out any repair.

YOU WILL NEED

- Hot air gun
- Jeweller's hammer
- Brass rod
- Solvent
- Silver rod
- Pliers
- Piercing saw
- Files
- Solder
- Large round stake or something round to tap on
- Flux

- Small self-igniting gas torch
- Pendant drill, abrasive tools and mops
- Pitch and pitch pan
- Silver wire
- Hammer
- Level engineer's plate
- Mirror glass
- Soft iron wire
- Rolling mill
- Wire wool

The finished repair

ASSESSING THE CHALLENGE

This Art Nouveau mirror arrived with both the mirror glass and bezel to hold it in place missing; and also with damage to a lot of the decoration. In particular, the main face of the character in the handle is badly mangled.

It is quite common with filled items like this mirror for the high points of the decoration to be worn away. They are the first point of contact when the mirror is put down and the highest, most vulnerable point when the metal is polished. The character's nose has literally been worn away and there are a number of dents to both the back and front of the handle, including the character's cheek. The biggest problem is that the dents are at the bottom of the handle, where there is poor access.

Before you begin, order your replacement glass at the appropriate size from your supplier. In this case 2mm thickness is used. I'm using plain mirror glass here, but if you prefer, the glass can be bevelled by some suppliers, which gives a pleasant look.

Hallmark

This detail shows the sponsor's mark of AE Goodby and Son on the left. On the right, the anchor shows this mirror was assayed in Birmingham, the world's largest assay office. The material – sterling silver – is indicated by the lion in an octagon metal fineness mark. Finally, the lower-case 'h' with this shape of border is the date mark, indicating this mirror was assayed in 1907.

A common issue with filled silver items is denting, and this is often caused by small air pockets in the filler material. These air pockets are hidden below the thin silver surface and, as these areas are unsupported by the filler material, even light pressure can dent the silver. This is exactly what has happened to the face on this handle. The nose has been crushed, and the cheek has sustained a blow and become dented.

This detail shows the filler behind the broken mirror glass. You can also see the wooden stick that runs down the handle and behind the glass to support the centre of the mirror.

Removing the loose pitch.

Suspending the mirror like this means that gravity will do the work for you as the pitch melts.

REMOVING THE PITCH

The first thing to do is to remove the pitch filler. The visible pitch behind the lost glass can be carefully broken up with a hammer, but It is impossible to chip away the pitch inside the hollow handle, and it therefore needs to be melted out. Good ventilation is paramount, so do this stage outside if possible, and into a metal container.

- Use a jeweller's hammer to chip away the loose bits of bitumen very delicately and gradually. Be careful not to damage the very thin silver below.
- Suspend the mirror with soft iron wire so that the handle is upright. Heat it gently and slowly with a paint stripping type hot air gun until the pitch begins to flow.
- While the pitch is soft, pull the stick that runs down the handle out of the mirror and put it to one side, then continue heating with the hot air gun.
- Once all the pitch has melted out of the mirror and it has cooled down, clean the residue out using a solvent such as acetone, thinners or white spirit. This is very dirty work and protective gloves should be worn.
- Once the mirror handle is clean, repair work can commence. Make sure there is no pitch left on the area to be repaired or the outside of the mirror. A little remaining in the cavities inside is fine, as it will be refilled later.

Cleaning with solvent.

Ready for repair.

FIXING DENTS IN FILLED SILVER

To remove the dents in the handle, a tool needs to be made to lever out each dent from inside. Through careful measurement and closely observing the shape, a bespoke implement can be constructed to work perfectly for the particular repair in hand.

Plan what you need the tool to do in order to choose the right material. Here, the tool needs to be long enough to fit down the handle, and strong enough to force the silver outwards. I've chosen to use brass rod of 6mm (¼in) diameter, as this is rigid enough to work.

- Use pliers to bend the tip of the brass rod slightly, then use a file to round off any sharp edges – this is to avoid puncturing or unintentionally distorting the thin silver layer. A fine but blunt end is perfect for giving the roundness in the cheek.

- Measure the length of the mirror's handle, and put another bend in the rod, a short distance beyond the length of the handle. This will give you a little wiggle room – quite literally – to manoeuvre the tool.

- Slip the tool down the hollow handle. By twisting and manipulating while carefully watching the action from the outside, raise the dent in the back of the handle.

- Turn the tool inside the handle, and raise the cheek on the front to its correct profile in the same way. If you accidentally take it slightly too high, don't worry – it can be moved back down later.

The completed dent-removing tool, and a detail of the rounded-off tip.

Raising the dent with a specially made brass tool. Fixing the relatively larger and simpler dent here will give you a feel for how the tool works before turning to the more delicate cheek on the other side.

Raising cheek dent with specially made brass tool.

CREATING THE NOSE

The next task is to make a nose from solid silver that can sit in the void in the character's face. This can be quite hard to make it look correct – and it may take a few attempts to avoid the person looking like Pinocchio.

The nose will need to be soldered into place. Because the silver (of the handle) is so thin, a low melting temperature tin/silver solder is chosen to attach the replacement nose. Higher melting temperature silver solder could damage the incredibly thin body of the mirror.

- Hold a short piece of silver wire – I'm using 4mm square wire – in a pair of parallel action pliers. Use a flat file to gradually file it down until it resembles a nose that will fit in the hole.
- Try the nose in place and observe, then make adjustments until you are satisfied that it looks right.

Carving a nose from silver using a file.

Trying the new nose for size.

ATTACHING THE NOSE

Once you are happy with the nose, it can be soldered into place.

- Apply flux to the area to be soldered – this will help the solder to flow and keep the joint clean.
- Apply a small pallion of solder to the area, then heat the joint with the small self-igniting propane torch. If there is not enough solder, more can be added. It should be noted that is easier to add more solder than it is to remove an excess.
- Once soldering is complete the edges of the joint can be cleaned and polished, firstly with a pointed abrasive wheel, then polishing mops.

Fluxing the joint.

Placing the solder pallion into position.

Soldering the nose into place.

Cleaning and smoothing the soldered joint.

Heating the pine pitch.

REFILLING

Once the nose is in place, polished and you are happy that all of the dents are removed, the mirror can be re-filled with pitch. Naturally, the variety I have chosen is the pleasant-smelling pine pitch (see 'Secrets of filled silver', below). As it slowly warms, the distinctive, welcome fragrance of a pine forest emerges.

Work carefully here, and keep an eye out for bubbles. If the pitch sets with any unseen air pockets, the surrounding area will be very vulnerable to denting as there is no support from behind.

- Wearing protective gloves, warm the pitch using the hot air paint stripper, then replace the wooden stick, saved earlier, into the handle.
- Lay the mirror flat and pour the hot pitch into the mirror. It is important to keep warming the whole silver frame, including the handle, until all of the bubbles have stopped coming out. You may need to tilt up a little to help the pitch to flow all the way down into the handle.
- Once you are satisfied there are no hidden air pockets, lay the mirror flat, continue warming until the pitch is level, then leave it to cool.

Pouring the hot pitch.

SECRETS OF FILLED SILVER

Pitch is the most common filler for thin gauge metal decorative items. More rarely, plaster is used, and this can crack as it has is no flexibility. To remove plaster, soak the piece in water for twenty-four hours and it should come out. On occasion, the item will have been repaired before and other glues or resins will have been used. This can cause severe problems as the correct solvent needs to be found.

There are two types of pitch used for filling silver. One is bitumen pitch, a black material used in making tarmacadam for roads. The other is pine pitch, made from tree resin. While pine pitch can be yellow or tan, it can also be black, making it hard to tell which type of pitch a piece is filled with – that is, until you heat it up. The resulting smell is instantly recognizable. As soon as this mirror was heated, this pitch began to smell, very distinctively, like roadworks – identifying it as bitumen pitch.

If one of your repairs turns out to be filled with the fresh, natural-smelling pine pitch, it is worth saving to use again, as I have in this project. Bitumen pitch, however, is best discarded.

The pitch levels itself as it cools, so make sure the mirror is held perfectly flat and still.

Using a rolling mill to flatten silver wire.

Curving the bezel wire.

MAKING THE BEZEL

The dimensions of the bezel wire are not critical – you simply need to ensure there is room between the top face of the mirror glass and the recess for the bezel in the frame. Here I'm using 0.7 x 3mm sterling silver wire for the bezel wire.

- Use a rolling mill to roll the round silver wire into a flat strip of the desired dimensions – you need enough to go all the way round the edge of the mirror surround, plus a little spare.
- Use a pair of parallel pliers to bend the flattened wire into the shape of the mirror surround.
- The bezel wire is made perfectly round by very gently taping its edge on a round stake. This has to be done slowly and with care, as it is easy to bend the thin edge of the bezel over.

This round stake is a specialized tool that will help to make the bezel wire a perfect round shape.

SILVERSMITHS SECRET

When rounding things like wire, you'll have an easier time if you can find an existing object of the right size to work round. Look for a empty gas bottle, empty fire extinguisher, round metal gatepost, part of a scrap car... anything you can find that is round, hard and roughly the right diameter.

Work very gently indeed when refining the sides of the bezel, as the bezel is edge-up.

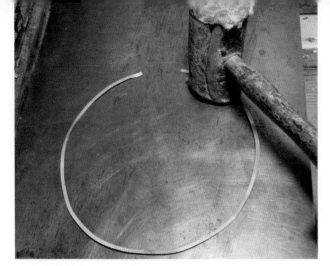

Flattening the bezel.

Soldering the bezel.

REPLACING THE GLASS

The ends of the bezel have been left too long deliberately – we now trim it to fit and secure the glass to finish.

- Once formed into a circle of the right size, the plane – that is, the front – of the bezel needs to be flattened. Place the bezel on an engineer's level bench plate, then use a hide mallet to tap it perfectly flat.

- Place the bezel loosely in the mirror and mark the ends.

- Cut the bezel with the piercing saw so that the finished circle fits very tightly in to its recess. When it is a complete circle it will lock into place.

- Remove the bezel from the mirror. Solder the two ends together using silver solder and borax flux (see soldering, pages 60–63) to finish the bezel.

- Sand down the surface with fine wet and dry paper until all of the marks are removed or you have the finish you want. In this example, I gave the bezel a brushed finish using fine wire wool.

- Place the mirror glass on the pitch. If it wobbles, stabilize it by placing a small piece of folded tissue paper behind the mirror at the 'low point' to level it.

- Once the glass is level, gently push the bezel into its slot to hold the mirror in place.

- Give the silver a final hand polish, clean the glass of any fingerprints, and the job is complete.

The finished repair can be seen on page 115.

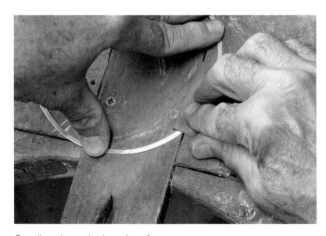

Sanding down the bezel surface.

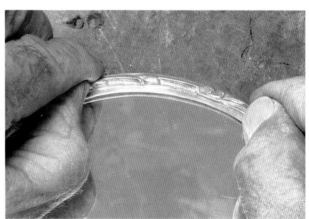

Pushing the securing bezel into place.

▶ **ITEM** Sterling silver pepper grinder, made by Alfred Dunhill, 1970, London.

▶ **AIM** Remove a large flat dent on base, and service the grinding mechanism.

▶ **DIFFICULTY OF REPAIR** Medium.

Before

YOU WILL NEED

- Screwdriver
- Leather sandbag
- Collet hammer
- Planishing hammer
- Files
- Wet and dry boards

- Correct stakes
- Engineer's bench vice
- Polishing equipment

The finished repair

ASSESSING THE CHALLENGE

Externally, this pepper pot has a large dent as a result of being dropped, knocking the circular base out of round. On the inside, the grinding mechanism no longer functions correctly.

My natural inquisitiveness means that if a mechanical item is serviceable (in this case the screws indicate that) I will always open it up to see how it works and what is going on. It can be useful to take pictures as you disassemble something, so you know how it is meant to go back together.

There is no manual for a pepper pot like this – you just need to look inside and see. If parts are missing, it may be possible to find a similar mechanism on an auction site or in a bric-a-brac shop.

Bottom of pepper pot showing the 'flat'.

Hallmark

A London-assayed piece, as indicated by the uncrowned leopard's head mark; the standard mark shows this pepper pot is sterling silver. The florid 'p' in an octagon shows it was assayed in 1970, and the maker's mark belongs to Alfred Dunhill & Sons.

Starting to strip down the mechanism.

All of the components have been removed from the pepper grinder.

FIXING THE DENT

The first task is to strip the pepper grinder down to its bare components. This will give access to the silver casing and allow the mechanical parts to be serviced.

- Use a screwdriver to loosen the screws underneath. If the screws will not come undone, try to tighten the screw a tiny bit before trying to undo it.
- Carefully take all of the components out and put all parts into a lidded container and label it. You may not return to the item for some time and it is easy to lose bits or forget what they are.
- Working on top of a leather sandbag (to protect the outside of the casing from getting scratched), begin to tap the dented area outwards using a curved collet hammer.
- Keep checking the shape to see the progress. The metal on this grinder is very thick due to the application of a decorative band at the base. It needs a great deal of force to re-shape and re-align.

Tapping the dent out using the collet hammer.

Check the shape regularly.

FINESSING THE BASE

Once the base is nearly round, a suitable stake needs to be found or made to insert into the base to refine the shape more precisely. In this case, a piece of brass was roughly tapered in a lathe to match the taper of the pepper pot itself, and fitted tightly into the base.

- Secure the stake in an engineer's bench vice.
- Fit the base over the stake.
- Use a flat planishing hammer, tapping around the base evenly; the circular form slowly returns.

Fitting the base over the brass stake held in the vice.

Gently planishing around the base.

A brief visual check will reveal whether it is round again.

CLEANING AND REASSEMBLY

Before reassembly, the pepper pot needs to be brought back to a sparkling finish, and the grinding parts of the mechanism need to be cleaned and sharpened, as in this case they were extremely dull.

- Any hammer marks left from the planishing need to be filed out using a flat fine file.
- Following this, use a piece of wet and dry paper wrapped around a flat wooden stick to remove the file marks.
- Following the instructions on page 69, polish the pepper pot.
- Run a square needle file along the grooves to clear them and give a cutting edge back to the grinding mechanism.
- Once the male and female parts are cleaned, the mechanism can be reassembled.
- Fill the pepper pot with peppercorns, then try it out.

Filing away the hammer marks.

Removing file marks with wet and dry paper.

The finished repair can be seen on page 125.

Cleaning and sharpening the grooves of the mechanism.

▶ **ITEM** Sterling silver picture frame by Joseph and Richard Griffin, Chester, date unclear: possibly 1909.

▶ **AIM** To replace missing corners.

▶ **DIFFICULTY OF REPAIR** Medium.

The first thing that should be understood about some picture and mirror frames is that they are made from very thin silver that has been stamped in a mould to apply the decoration. Silversmiths could make fancy hallmarked goods at a relatively low material cost by using thin silver.

Such items were often decorated by pressing a raised, embossed, pattern into the silver. As well as being decorative, this also gives the metal an inherent strength because a curved structure has more strength than a flat structure of the same gauge of metal.

Despite this, such pieces are still inherently frail and, if they are over-polished, the highest parts can actually wear through. Likewise, large raised areas without pattern, such as the bulge at the top of this frame, could easily be flattened with a thumb or finger pressure. While that has not happened here, you can see another common problem – the corners have broken off.

Before

YOU WILL NEED

- Scissors
- Pliers – both round-nosed and flat-nosed
- Doming punch
- Engineer's flat plate/block
- Hammer
- Solder/flux
- Titanium or aluminium sheet
- Titanium or tungsten probe
- Polish
- Burr, scraper or needle file
- Small self-igniting gas torch

The finished repair

ASSESSING THE CHALLENGE

The silver used for this frame is just 0.25mm thick. Three of the four corners have got caught when polishing and then, due to metal fatigue, broken off.

The task here is to recreate a corner that will fit in almost seamlessly with the overall design. The ideal scenario would be to remove all of the pins holding the metal to the wooden base so the silver could have been worked upon separately.

Unfortunately, in this instance the wood is oak, which gripped the pin-heads so tightly that they just snapped off when I attempted to remove them. They have been in the wood for over a hundred years and that's where these ones are staying. The repairs will need to be carried out with the silver *in situ*.

Detail of the damaged corner

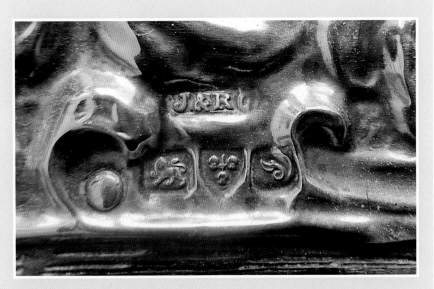

Hallmark

The florid 'I' marks this as a 1909 piece. The lion indicates it is sterling silver, while the three wheat sheaves and sword device shows it was assayed in the Chester Assay Office, which was closed in 1962. The maker's mark is unfortunately unclear, but it is likely to be that of J & R Griffin, silversmiths of Birmingham.

MAKING THE CORNERS

After observing the corner, I decided it was best to make a raised area where the converging edges meet. There is a raised edge on both sides that also needs matching with the original outside edge.

It is always good if recycled silver can be used for repairing. I looked through my scrap silver container and found a piece of hallmarked silver of the correct thickness from an old hairbrush backing. This can be re-purposed for repairing the frame.

Once a corner is cut, it needs to be slipped under the original metal and a rough line scribed or delineated to match.

- The first objective is to raise the corner. This is done with a doming punch on the leather sandbag.

- Next the raised lines on the edges need to be formed. Using round-nosed and flat-nosed pliers together, an edge can be bent over. Do not worry that the corner does not appear correct at this stage.

- Once the edges are created, the corner needs to be placed on a flat engineer's block. The centre part needs to pushed down level with the block. The raised edges and corner will help to facilitate this due to their strength. An extra small doming punch mark was added at this stage; a further disguise to prevent the eye being drawn to the repair.

Cutting a new corner from scrap silver. The silver is so thin from the old hairbrush that it can be cut with ordinary scissors.

Marking the size of the replacement corner.

Raising the corner with the doming punch.

A detail of the domed corner.

Making an edge with round- and flat-nosed pliers.

Pushing the centre of the corner level.

Cleaning under the silver prior to soldering.

PREPARING THE CORNERS

Place each corner onto the silver frame and make any tweaks and adjustments that are needed. It is not imperative that it is absolutely identical to the original – the idea is just to fool the eye that the corner is as it was when the frame was first made.

- Once it looks good to the eye, clean underneath gently using a burr, scraper or needle file.
- The next step is to ease a thin piece of titanium or aluminium sheet under the corner to avoid the wood getting contaminated with flux, and to stop it burning. (The solder will not adhere to these backing metals.) Slip the new corner under the original silver and line it up.
- Add flux to ensure a good solder joint occurs.

The corner in position, ready for soldering.

Fluxing prior to soldering.

ATTACHING THE CORNERS

A small pallion of Staybrite solder is cut and placed on the joint. I advise using this sort of solder here, as silver solder has to be heated to such a temperature that it would burn the wood backing.

- Gently heat the area with a small torch; the flux boils first.
- Make a final check that everything is lined up; then polish by hand to finish.

Melting the solder pallion. The frame is being held in a level plane with the corner with a tungsten probe.

SILVERSMITHS SECRETS: SOLDERING

- *When the flux boils, check that it hasn't dislodged the pallion or the joint. Boiling the flux when soft soldering is an indication that the solder is about to flow.*
- *Tungsten probes can be home-made from discarded TIG welding electrodes.*

The finished repair can be seen on page 131.

Before

▶ **ITEM** Sterling silver pin cushion. Maker unknown, date unknown, town unknown.

▶ **AIM** Replace cushion and repair sharp edge that scratches furniture.

▶ **DIFFICULTY OF REPAIR** Easy.

Many silver items with a practical use are made of multiple parts, some of which may degrade or get lost over time. This pincushion is an excellent example of a perfectly serviceable piece that just needs a replacement cushion – and a baize base to stop it scuffing the surface it's placed on.

Some of the techniques shown here could be used on watch stand bases, inkwells and paperweights. Applying felt to the bottom of a piece is a skill that will brighten up anything that does not get wet and will save furniture from getting scratched.

YOU WILL NEED

- Cork sheet
- Felt-tip pen
- Glue
- Scissors
- Piercing saw
- Lathe (optional) or potter's decoration wheel

- Sandpaper
- Clamps
- Scalpel
- Sticky-backed baize
- Double-sided tape
- Cotton velvet
- Craft knife

The finished repair

ASSESSING THE CHALLENGE

The main silver work here is to make sure that the pin cushion's base no longer scratches the furniture. We'll also need to replace the cushion. Although not strictly a silver repair, pin cushions and hat pin cushions are often in need of attention.

Pin cushions are often small bags that are sewn up with a granular or soft material encased. These materials can be ground walnut, rice, plastic beads, fabric or even wire wool which stuff the cushion. In this pin cushion, I believe that the material inside the cushion was originally cork, as there was evidence of glue and cork on top of the wooden spacer.

The wooden spacer holds the cork level with the top of the silver, so the whole of the pin cushion is not full of cork.

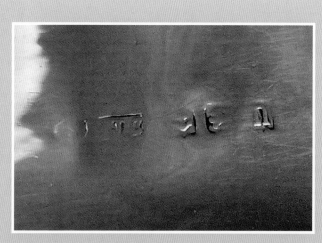

Hallmark

This piece has been 'rubbed' – that is, over-polished, and so the hallmark is so unclear as to be almost illegible. The second mark in from the right looks like the remnants of an anchor, so it may have been assayed in Birmingham. If this was the case, the remnants of the 'm' date letter on the right suggest it was made in 1911.

To the left of this, the remnants of a lion hint that this is sterling silver. The maker's mark is the most badly rubbed, and my best guess is that it was made by Thomas James Skelton, who worked from Vyse Street, Birmingham, between 1903 and 1915 – although he seems to have had most of his work assayed in Chester, so this is far from certain.

CREATING THE DOME

We can use the original wooden spacer as the template for the cork we need to fill the space.

- With some reconstituted cork sheets and a felt-tip pen, mark the circle size.
- Use a piercing saw to cut out these discs, making them slightly larger than the hole in the holder.
- Glue the cork discs together using PVA wood glue, and glue them to the round wooden base. Place the stack in a vice or clamp and leave to dry.

Drawing around the spacer to ensure the cork circles are the right size.

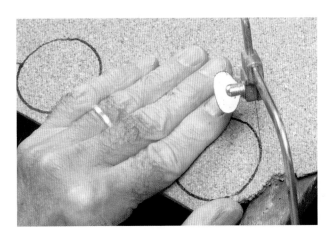

Cutting out circles from the cork.

SILVERSMITHS SECRETS: SAWING

- *Saw vertically using the piercing saw in a similar manner to cutting metal (see page 56). Try not to angle the blade forward, as you'll find it harder to stay on the line.*
- *If you are cutting non-precious material – as with the cork here – unhook the bench skin to allow the sawdust/filings to fall to the floor. This avoids contaminating the precious metal lemel.*

Clamped in position.

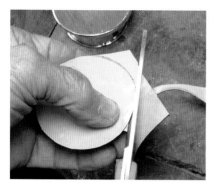

Using the base as a template, mark the back of the baize, then cut out the shape.

Removing the backing from the baize.

The baize backing in place.

ADDING THE BAIZE

While the glue is setting, baize can be applied to the base of the holder. Baize comes on a roll which you cut and glue or a sticky backed version is available too. In this case, the latter is being used.

- Mark the size of the wooden bottom of the item and cut around with scissors. It is tricky to cut as the glue layer can bind a bit with the scissors.
- Remove the backing and apply to the wooden base of the pin cushion. It is important to get it lined up correctly as it does not like to be removed once stuck down – the adhesive is incredibly strong.
- Once the glue has dried, the cork needs to be domed. Use double-sided tape to temporarily attach the wood to a potter's decoration wheel or soldering turntable, then use sandpaper to shape the cork layers into an even dome.

SECRETS OF BAIZE

If the base is not a true round or an awkward shape, the baize can be stuck to the base first and then can be cut using a scalpel around the edge.

Care must be taken not to scratch or cut the item with the scalpel.

DOMING WITH A LATHE

If you have the luxury of a lathe, the cork dome can be fashioned on it. The tool needs to be extremely sharp and the lathe has to be rotating at its highest speed.

Once roughly right, the dome is sanded in place by rotating the chuck by hand. This should never be attempted with the lathe running: the risk of injury is quite high.

Doming the cork on a lathe.

Sanding dome with lathe inactive.

Double-sided tape being put on the wooden spacer.

COVERING AND FITTING THE DOME

Covering the dome with velvet will provide the finishing touch.

- Once the dome is the correct size stick some double-sided tape to the top of the wooden spacer.
- Next cut a piece of cotton velvet of the chosen colour and place it in your hand 'good side' down.
- Place the cork into your cupped hand and gently pick up the material, pleating it and sticking it to the double-sided tape.
- If the pleats become too thick (so that the whole thing will not insert into the silver holder), use a craft knife to cut them away below the bottom edge of the dome, where it doesn't show.
- Once the dome is smoothed and even, it can be fitted to the silver to finish. It is a friction fit and does not need to be glued in place.

Placing the cork onto the material.

Trimming the pleats.

Checking the final fitting.

The finished repair can be seen on page 137.

▶ **ITEM** Sterling silver coffee pot, maker J. Parkes & Co, London, 1933

▶ **AIM** Remove dent and generally clean up and restore.

▶ **DIFFICULTY OF REPAIR** Easy

This coffee pot is an example of hollowware; that is, an object that holds something inside due to the nature of its design. Similar common hollowware items are goblets, teapots, vases and bowls. They are normally dented from the outside and the dent needs to be addressed from the inside. So as long as you can get access, you should be able to remove the dent. Problems occur when, for example, there is a dent in a hollow handle that is soldered on.

Before

YOU WILL NEED

- Round stake
- Vice
- Planishing hammer
- Fine flat file
- Leather sand bag
- Water of Ayr stone or wet and dry boards

- Polishing machine and ancillaries
- Polish
- Wire wool
- Wax polish
- Cloth

The finished repair

ASSESSING THE CHALLENGE

This coffee pot has sustained a large dent on its side. Fortunately, the dent is right on the side and the side of the pot is straight – this means we can fix it using a stake.

A large and obvious dent ruins the visual appeal of this piece – but since the damage hasn't punctured the surface, it'll be easy to make good.

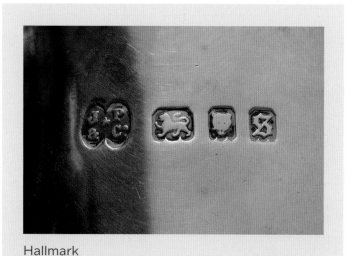

Hallmark

A clear hallmark here makes identification easy. This sterling silver pot, made by J. Parkes & Co., was assayed in London in 1933.

REMOVING THE DENT WITH A STAKE

You need a stake that fits snugly into the neck of the pot, so choose a stake with as large a diameter as possible while still fitting into the pot.

By placing the pot over the stake and gently moving back and forwards, the dent can be felt and the centre of the dent point on the stake can be located. The end of the stake is very slightly curved to avoid the creation of sharp marks.

- Start by clamping a straight round stake in a large vice.

- Line up the dent with the top of the stake and start to slide the coffee pot onto the stake. Imagine putting your hand inside the pot to feel the dent: the stake is acting like your hand finding the dent, its shape and its depth.

- Gently push down on the contact point while observing from above. The dent will be seen to rise back up to the correct original plane of the pot's side. Slowly and measuredly does it.

Stake in the clamp, ready to be used to remove the dent

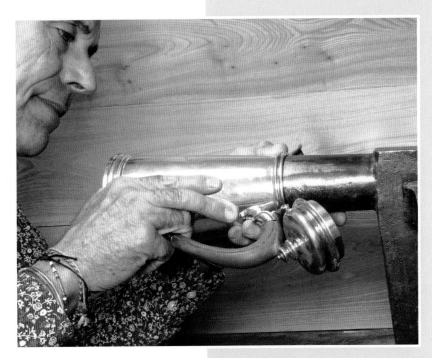

By creating a downwards pressure, the dent can be raised.

145

PLANISHING

Once the side of the pot is nearly correct and true, a few ripples will remain. This is normal, it would be almost impossible for this internal 'burnishing' to leave the surface perfect. It is at this point that the pot needs to be planished.

The smallest, flattest, highly-polished planishing hammer should be used to make the smallest, most delicate marks on the silver.

- Lay the pot on the stake; this ensures that it is flat to the metal.
- Very gently planish around the area, overlapping the facets, using the softest of taps.

Starting to planish on the stake.

Gentle, even planishing is the key to a good result.

SECRETS OF PLANISHING

Planishing leaves distinctive faint marks, which I polish away from the outside. I always, however, leave the planishing marks inside my silver work, as it is a beautiful feature of handmade silver. If you look, for instance, inside a Hester Bateman piece of hollowware you will see or feel the planishing.

Planishing must be done with care, because if you 'over' planish, a bulge will be created. This is hard to overcome and rectify and needs to be avoided. Find a position that is comfortable and work methodically and evenly.

Hammered pot ready to file. Note the faint circular planishing marks.

REFINING THE SURFACE

Once the damaged area is planished, the delicate hammer marks need to be filed out, and then the file marks smoothed. You can use wet and dry boards for this, but to show an alternative, I'm using a Water of Ayr stone.

The advantage of these stones is that they remove only the high points and do not ride down the furrows. The stone wears to the profile of the surface that is being 'stoned', which results in a fine surface that can be polished directly.

- Using a very fine file, file the tops of the hammer marks until the surface is smooth. Follow the curve and keep the file flat to the surface.

- To remove the file marks, wet the stone and press quite hard while running it over the surface; first up and down the pot, then around its curve. Any furrows left will manifest as a ripple when the silver is polished.

- Use a machine to polish the damaged area, then polish the whole pot by hand using a quality silver polish and a soft cloth.

- Rub down the fruit wood handle gently with wire wool (0000 grade). Take care not to scratch the silver sockets.

- To finish, wax the handle with a good-quality wax, then buff with a soft cloth.

Filing the hammer marks out.

Stoning the file marks and smoothing the surface.

Final polish by hand.

Waxing the handle after rubbing it down with wire wool.

SECRETS OF POLISHING

Avoid polishing the hallmark directly as the detail will wears away over time – a perfect example of how a hallmark can be rubbed is shown on page 138.

The finished repair can be seen on page 143.

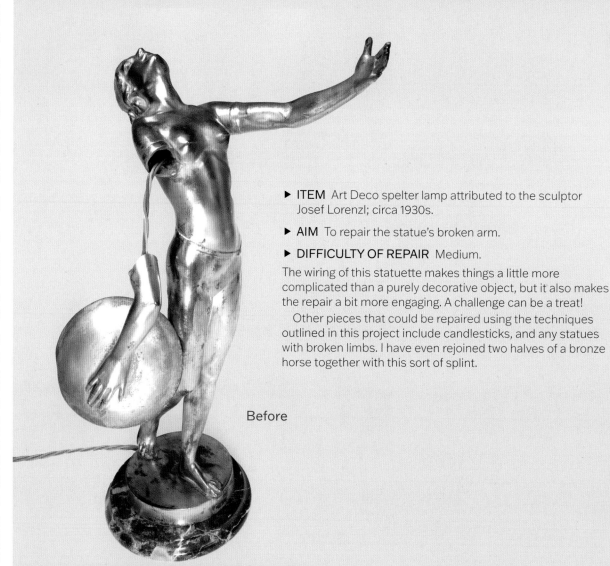

Before

▶ **ITEM** Art Deco spelter lamp attributed to the sculptor Josef Lorenzl; circa 1930s.

▶ **AIM** To repair the statue's broken arm.

▶ **DIFFICULTY OF REPAIR** Medium.

The wiring of this statuette makes things a little more complicated than a purely decorative object, but it also makes the repair a bit more engaging. A challenge can be a treat!

Other pieces that could be repaired using the techniques outlined in this project include candlesticks, and any statues with broken limbs. I have even rejoined two halves of a bronze horse together with this sort of splint.

YOU WILL NEED

- Snips
- Round bar
- Vice
- Brass sheet (0.8mm thick)
- Vernier gauge
- Soldering torch
- Soft solder and flux
- Piercing saw
- Hammer/mallet

- Fishing line (optional/as necessary)
- Screwdriver
- Files
- Pendant drill and accessories
- JB Weld two-part metal epoxy adhesive
- Milliput two-part epoxy putty
- Silver paint and paintbrush
- Black patinating wax and cloth
- Hairdryer/hot air gun (optional)

The finished repair

ASSESSING THE CHALLENGE

Unfortunately, the arm of the lady lamp-cum-statue has broken just by the bicep cuff. It is possible that these statues were cast with separate arms for ease of manufacturing, hence the cuffs to hide the join; this design created a weak point.

The combination of the lamp holder, bulb and globe makes a substantial weight supported by this small, delicate limb, so perhaps it is not surprising that a blow has caused it to break.

Detail of the join between arm and body.

REMOVING THE FLEX

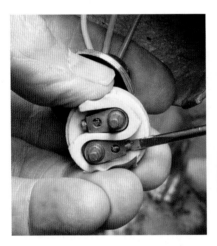

Undoing the wires.

Soldering a draw wire.

This particular lamp has recently been rewired with a current specification flex and an earth wire has been attached to the metal lamp holder. This means that the whole metal body of the lamp is earthed and therefore safe.

This flex needs to be removed to enable the repair to take place. Before doing this, a thinner 'draw' wire should be soldered to the original flex to allow the cables to be pulled through the arm. The draw wire cannot be taped as it might detach halfway through. Soldering is the solution.

- The first task is to remove the bulb holder. Undo the ring that holds the bulb holder in place
- Draw the ceramic or plastic connector out and disconnect the wires.
- Twist the copper core of the draw wire together.
- Offer some soft fluxed solder to it and solder the thin draw wire to the three parts of the flex.

SILVERSMITH'S SECRET

If the flex has already been removed, drop some fishing line with a small weight attached down the shoulder aperture. By manipulating the body and the weight, the line can be brought out at the aperture in the base – just like a Christmas cracker agility test! Next, tie a thin wire to the fishing line and draw it back through the body. Finally, solder the three stripped wires of a new electrical flex together onto the wire you have just drawn through the statue's body. The flex can then be carefully pulled up through the body.

Measuring the diameter of the inside of the arm.

CREATING A SPLINT

Next you need to create a tubular brass splint that fits into the upper and lower parts of the arm. Make sure that the two parts of the arm fit together without any gaps before you begin this stage.

- Use the vernier gauge to measure the diameter of the inside of the arm.
- Multiply this dimension by three and cut some brass – it was around 40 x 60mm (1½ x 2⅜in) in this case. This does not need to be too accurate as final adjustments will need to be made once the tube is made.
- Bend the brass over a round steel stake/former, held in a vice. This may become too hard to bend the edges inwards, so tap with a soft face hammer to close the gap and then tap to overlap the edges.
- If necessary because the tube is too large, you can adjust it by cutting a slice out of it with a piercing saw before making the curve true by tapping it with the soft-face hammer on the round bar again.
- It is important to test the fit of the tubular splint in both parts of the statuette to make sure it fits snugly. Any adjustments to the fit need to be made before moving on.

Cutting the brass with snips.

Bending the brass over a round stake.

Tapping the edges with a soft-faced hammer.

Using a piercing saw to make the tube smaller to fit.

Checking the fit of the tube in the arm and shoulder.

SOLDERING AND PREPARING THE JOINT

When you are happy with the size of the tube, this can be soldered with soft solder.

- Flux the joint and feed the solder from its stick onto the joint while gently heating the joint with the torch. The solder will flow along the small gap, and it will appear as a shiny line.

- Once the tube has cooled and the flux has been cleaned off, make sure that there are no sharp edges that could chafe the flex. Feed the wire that protrudes from the shoulder through the tube and then through the arm up into the area where the lamp holder sits. This can be a bit fiddly. Try one more time 'dry' fitting, that is, without any adhesive.

- Take the tube back out and file the outside of it as roughly as possible with the coarsest file available. This will 'key' the metal and help the adhesive stick.

- Clean up inside the arm and shoulder spaces or voids using a pendant drill and small sanding drum, again this all helps adhesion. Be careful of the flex.

Adding flux to the joint with a paintbrush.

Soldering the joint.

Dry fitting the join after feeding the wire through.

Cleaning and abrading the area to be glued with a coarse file and then a pendant drill.

SECURING THE ARM IN POSITION

Make sure the arm looks correct and that the tube isn't pushing it out of line. Once happy, it's time to glue the pieces and leave them to set in the correct position.

- Squeeze equal parts of the adhesive (I am using JB Weld) onto a scrap of wood and mix them together thoroughly.
- Start to load the adhesive onto the shoulder area between the statue's arm and the tubular splint. Fill all the gaps, but avoid getting any adhesive on the flex.
- Put adhesive onto the tube and into the arm, again being careful to avoid getting it on the flex. Push the two parts together, at the same time taking up slack in the flex by pulling the draw wire.
- Use supports such as tape to hold the repaired joint securely in the correct position, then leave overnight to set.

SILVERSMITH'S SECRET

Practise securing at the dry assembly stage (i.e. without any adhesive) to make sure that the materials and arrangement you use to hold it will work.

Never apply tape directly to a plated spelter piece. The substrate is likely to fail and when you remove the tape, the colour will come off with it.

Mixing the two-part adhesive to a uniform colour.

Using a scrap of metal to apply adhesive to the splint and into the shoulder and arm voids.

Gently easing the arm into the shoulder for the final time.

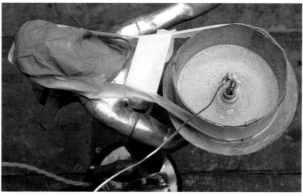

Using tape to hold the arm securely in place to dry. Note the use of an old glove to protect the silver plating from the adhesive tape.

DISGUISING THE JOIN

We now need to disguise the join from the outside. The join on this arm has worked really well and it hardly needs any filling – if your repair is more extreme, you may need more – but be careful not to add too much putty at once. By making a thin thread, the amount of putty being introduced can be easily controlled.

- Wearing protective gloves, mix equal parts of two-part Milliput or equivalent epoxy putty.

- Once mixed thoroughly, roll a piece of the mixed putty under your fingers on a flat surface to make a thin 'thread'.

- Carefully wrap the thread around the join line. There is plenty of working time to perfect this as the putty remains supple for over thirty minutes under normal conditions.

- Use a damp cloth to smooth over the joint and leave the putty to fully cure. Clean any areas that may have been contaminated by putty at this stage, again using a damp cloth.

- This darker putty line can be coloured once set. Using a fine paintbrush and some silver or chrome paint to delicately cover the putty.

SECRETS OF EPOXY PUTTY

- *If the unmixed epoxy putty has gone hard after standing for a while after being opened, it can be resurrected by warming with a hot air gun. It makes it much more supple and easier to mix and apply.*

- *A hairdryer or hot air gun will reduce standard setting times significantly. Just warm the putty – not too hot.*

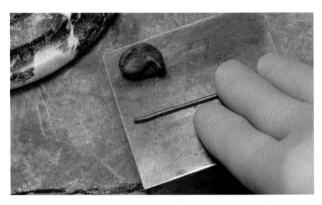

Rolling epoxy putty into a thin thread after mixing equal parts thoroughly.

Wrapping the putty thread around to cover the join.

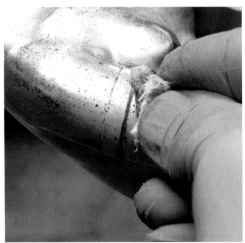

Smoothing the putty with a damp cloth.

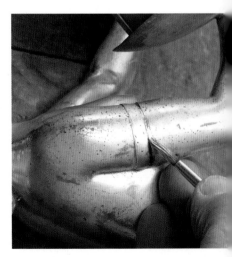

Colouring the line of dark putty with paint.

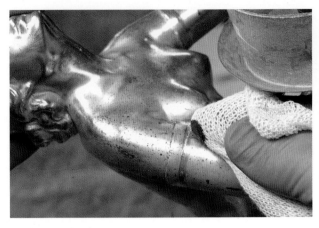

Applying patinating wax.

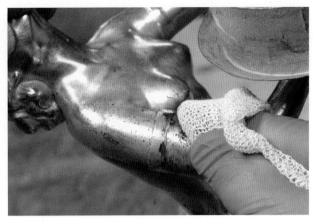

Working patinating wax into the area.

FINISHING TOUCHES

The lamp is now ready to be cleaned and rewired, ready for use.

- Once the paint has dried, put a small amount of black patinating wax onto a cloth and wipe around the joint to disguise its newness.

- Buff the whole area with a soft clean cloth.

- Finally, if you are not competent at wiring, get an electrician to rewire the lamp holder and check the whole lamp for safety.

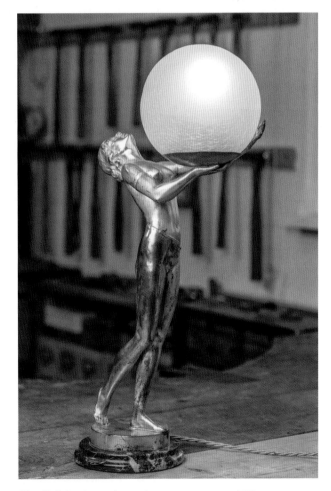

The finished repair can be seen on page 149.

Before

Item Statuette of a female dancer, gold-painted, circa early twentieth century, maker unknown.

Aim To repair the break at the ankle.

Difficulty of repair Easy.

Artists and sculptors regularly push the limits of the durability of the materials – often spelter, pewter or bronze – in the name of dynamism and giving their pieces impact. A figure standing on a single leg, balancing, or an animal rearing up on two legs are good examples of this. These sculptures are pleasing to the eye, but are vulnerable and susceptible to breakage at the weakest and narrowest point.

Often when these decorative figurines and animal sculptures are damaged, the results can be catastrophic. This example is a solid spelter figurine. She has a gold-painted finish. At some stage, I imagine that she has been dropped, and her weight against the large base has caused her foot to be severed at her ankle.

YOU WILL NEED

- Drill and bits
- Material to make pin: 25mm (1in) length of 1.75mm diameter steel
- Epoxy metal adhesive
- Parallel pliers
- Grade 0000 wire wool
- Epoxy putty
- Etch primer

- Gold paint and paintbrush
- Patinating/antiquing wax
- Scissors
- Card
- Baize
- Double-sided tape

The finished repair

The point of breakage.

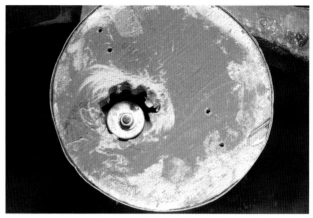

A previous repairer's attempt to reach the securing nut.

ASSESSING THE CHALLENGE

Wherever the break, the most important remedial action is to splint it before trying to rejoin the two parts; this will give the repaired joint sufficient strength to support the weight. A butt joint (where the two faces are simply placed together without any additional shaping or support) will simply not suffice.

We can see by looking at the base that someone has attempted a repair before using the rather unconventional method of repeatedly drilling the wooden inner base to reach her foot, which is bolted through the base. This problem can be addressed at the last stage of the repair.

ADDING A SPLINT

The splint can be made from a short length – 25mm (1in) or so – of 1.75mm diameter steel. A pop rivet nail, broken drill or hardened steel nail will all work. The important thing is that it is rigid and strong enough to support the weight of the statuette.

A suitable drill bit that matches the wire splint then needs to be found. A hand drill or cordless drill can be used. During this repair, a pendant drill with a foot-operated speed controller is being used. The flexible shaft, small hand grip and easily controllable speed make it the favoured choice.

Carefully drilling into the ankle.

- Carefully drill into the ankle where it joins the foot about 13mm (½in) in depth using a 1.75mm drill.

- Next, drill a matching hole up into the core of the shin. Great care should be take to line these holes up and, if possible, they should be near the centre of the leg for maximum strength.

- It can be helpful to measure using a pair of dividers to mark the positions of the corresponding spots.

Pushing the pin into the drilled hole.

Dry fitting to test to ensure the foot, splint and ankle will all line up.

- It is important to try the splint in the aperture using firstly a pair of parallel pliers to push one half in. Holding the rest of the sculpture carefully, push the two halves of the figure together.

- If the holes are drilled correctly the two parts will line up. This assembly of the figure 'dry' (i.e. without any adhesive) gives an indication of how the repair will look when the adhesive is added. In most cases, the figure should be able to stand without adhesive, the strength and tightness of the splint doing the main job of supporting.

- Now is the time for gluing. In this case we are using a two-part metal epoxy adhesive JB Weld. The glue is measured out equally and mixed thoroughly. It is important to wear protective gloves when mixing epoxy glues.

- Remove the splint, then apply glue into the holes where the wire will go and onto the two broken faces.

- Put the splint wire into one hole and push it in firmly, again with the parallel pliers.

- Fit the other part of the sculpture onto the splint and manoeuvre it into position. If it is not standing correctly adjust and support, then leave to dry. Generally speaking, the longer the setting time, the stronger the adhesive, but you can use the rapid ones if you wish.

Mixing the two-part metal epoxy glue.

Pressing the parts together once the glue has been added and splint replaced.

The glue should ooze from the joint, ensuring that there is enough to fill the whole gap.

DISGUISING THE JOIN

Even when the best join has been achieved, nine times out of ten it will still show, as the break is often not completely clean. You can address this by smoothing, then resculpting the joint.

- Work over the joint with a half-round file to remove any high spots, then file over the surrounding areas. This will clean up the repair and give the surface a 'key'. This key will help the putty to adhere in the next step.

- Mix an even amount of two-part Milliput epoxy putty thoroughly.

- Wet the join and keyed area by dipping your gloved finger in some water, then apply a small amount of putty.

- Work the putty into shape by smoothing it with your wetted finger, following the contours of the limb.

- Continue smoothing the edges of the putty where they meet the metal until the join is invisible and the surface is smoothed.

- Allow the joint to dry completely (probably overnight, but check the manufacturer's recommendations), then apply a 'high build' etch prime over the area using a paintbrush.

- Give the whole statuette a very light rubdown all over with wire wool (0000 grade) to give the top gold coat a key to attach itself to.

- Paint the statuette evenly and lightly all over to avoid unsightly runs and create a uniform finish.

Filing the joint.

A wet finger helps to smooth the putty. There is plenty of working time to do this, so no need to rush.

Repaired leg with perfect profile.

SECRETS OF MILLIPUT

- *Through wetting and smoothing, Milliput can be faded or feathered so thinly that there isn't a visible step or edge.*
- *It is possible to sand Milliput after it has cured. This allows you to refine the outer splint to the correct shape if necessary.*

Priming the repair. I used an aerosol primer intended for car paint repair, and squirted a tiny bit into a plastic container to use as a palette (do this outdoors). This allowed me to use it with a brush.

Touching up the repair with gold paint.

FINISHING

This paint can be left as-is or, if you prefer, a distressed antique finish can be applied using a black patinating wax. The wax sticks in the lower parts of the contours, simulating where dirt would naturally gather over time and creating contrast with the raised parts that remain highly polished gold. This gives the appearance of a much-loved and handled antique.

- Apply the patinating wax with a cloth, rubbing it in gently. Keep standing back and observing the colour until you judge it looks right.
- Once you are happy with the finish, re-bolt the statuette to its base.
- A baize disc can be fitted onto the base to cover the unsightly hole and protect furniture. Draw around the base onto stiff cardboard.
- Glue the baize to the card.
- Use scissors to cut out the shape of the base, then attach the resulting baize disc to the bottom of the statuette with double-sided tape.

Patinating wax is added to the repaired area.

Marking the shape of the base on card.

Attach the baize to the back of the card.

Cutting out the baize by trimming along the shape marked earlier.

SECRETS OF PATINATION

There is a plethora of antiquing waxes, paints and stains available to aid re-colouring of just about any metal sculpture. The key is to avoid a huge contrast between the repaired area and the original.

The finished repair can be seen on page 156.

AFTERWORD

Silversmithing is an ancient craft that has been practised for millennia. Like many other crafts, the skills to work it have been passed down through generations of adept artisans. This craft has produced some of the most beautiful and intricate objects that the world has ever seen. Used to make items as diverse as religious artefacts, ornate tea sets as decorative as they are practical, and even intricately-decorated weapons, silver – alongside many other metals – has long been used for both practical and artistic purposes.

In recent times, these crafts have become less common, as modern manufacturing techniques have made it easier to mass-produce metal objects. However, there is still a need, and significant demand, for skilled, practical and creative metalworkers and silversmiths. The art of these men and women continues to be appreciated by collectors and enthusiasts around the world.

I have written this book on silversmithing and small metal repair work as a resource for those interested in learning these crafts or improving their existing skills. I have aimed to cover a range of invaluable topics, including some of the history of silversmithing and metalwork; the techniques used to create and repair objects; and the tools and materials needed to do so.

One of the most important aspects of this book for me was to give the reader the insight and ability to understand the properties of the individual metals being used. As you have learned, each presents its own challenges and offers its own opportunities. Silver may be a soft and malleable metal that is easy to work with, but it is also prone to tarnishing and damage over time. Other metals, such as copper and bronze, likewise have their own unique properties that must be understood in order to create and repair objects effectively. Metals can bite back if they are not understood – pewter, for example, will melt when heated, causing catastrophic damage if not treated with the utmost caution and respect – and so I wanted to ensure that you are well-prepared and equipped to deal with any of the common metals you will find yourself working with.

I also judged it important to cover a range of the most important techniques to allow you to shape, join, and finish metal objects – and show how they are used in practice. The real world is rarely as neat as theory, and so showing you how burnishing, dent removal, soldering and other essential techniques are actually applied was foremost in my mind. Each and every item will have its own unique challenges, requiring just the right tools or materials. I have aimed to provide clear and broad instructions and illustrations for all of these, so that you can assess and decide what you will need for your own projects.

Most importantly, I wrote this book to pass on my experience and secrets; to inspire and give you the knowledge, skills and confidence to overcome any issues and solve any problems you find while fixing your items; and to become in the process another practical craftsperson.

Glossary

One last set of secrets. Silversmithing is packed with specialist terminology, often with interesting historical origins, and sometimes obscure. This glossary will help you with jargon-busting, and ensure you know just what to say when discussing a technique or looking for a tool.

Alloy A metal made by combining two or more elements. Sterling silver is an alloy of silver and (usually) copper, for example.

Annealing The process of heating hardened metal to a high temperature and letting it cool to relax the molecules in the structure. This makes the metal more malleable.

Anti-flux Mixed with water and painted near a joint, this will stop the solder flowing where it is applied. Yellow ochre watercolour paint makes excellent anti-flux.

Argotect A brand name for a flux which is painted onto the silver's surface before either annealing or soldering. It can help to reduce the build-up of firestain.

Arkansas stone A grey stone used for sharpening engravers' tools.

Assaying To test a precious metal for its quality.

Base metal Non-precious metal, such as copper or brass.

Bearer Bearers are the parts of the hinge that are attached to an opening lid and the part that the lid is hinged from. Typically, it has a half-round channel that holds the knuckles.

Benchpeg This is a wooden peg with a 'V' cut into it, used to support items when filing and especially piercing. The 'V' supports both sides of what is being cut.

Bezel A ring of wire that is used to hold a mirror in its frame, for example.

Binding This is the use of iron 'binding wire' to hold items in position when soldering.

Bright cut Refers to a decorative surface applied to a silver piece using a sharp, highly polished engraver. This patterned cutting causes attractive reflections and makes the surface almost sparkle.

Broach These are tapered sharp cutting tools. They are used for cleaning out and lining up hinge knuckles and to enlarge small holes. A broach is rolled between the thumb and fingers using its small round handle.

Burnishing To smooth metal using a highly polished tool. No metal is removed during the process. Quite deep scratches can be removed by burnishing.

Casting To introduce molten metal into a mould to make a copy of a pattern part.

Chasing and **repoussé** Techniques, usually involving using a hammer and punches, that create a raised, or relief pattern in a metal object. A decorative piece that has been so embellished can be describe as 'chased'.

Chenier Thin tube used for items that require hollow insides, such as jewellery hinges.

Crucible A ceramic vessel that metal is melted in and poured from. It can withstand the high temperatures required for making metal molten.

Dapping block and punches Another name for doming block and punches.

De-nib To remove imperfections ('nibs') from a surface after it has had a sealer, paint or polish applied. This is done usually with fine wire wool or sandpaper.

Ductility The ability of a metal to be drawn out into, say, a long wire without breaking.

Electro-plating By using precious metal liquid salts and a low voltage DC circuit, silver or gold are deposited on the surface of the item requiring plating. The longer this process is carried out, the thicker and more durable the coating.

Emery Either a paper or a cloth that has a silicon cutting compound glued to it for sanding purposes. It comes in various grades. See also wet and dry paper on page 38.

Ferrule A ring or cap made of metal that strengthens a stick.

Firestain or **Firescale** Copper is used as part of the sterling silver alloy, and this unwanted discoloration is an unfortunate by-product. Firestain is a tough layer of oxide containing copper that presents itself on the surface after heating. It needs to be abraded away using a file or wet and dry paper. I have found that when polishing old pieces, firestain sometimes becomes apparent – this tells me that the maker silver-plated the piece after polishing to disguise the acquired firestain. There are modern silver alloys that do not present firestain when they are heated.

Flatware A term that describes silver cutlery.

Forging A process where thick metal is hammered and shaped and annealed many times. Spoons and forks were often forged from a single block of silver. The item is not annealed after the last hammering process, leaving the item 'work hardened'.

Graver Another term for engraving tool.

Hardening To work an item that has been previously annealed or soldered causing it to become annealed. Hardening can be achieved by working the metal, typically by hammering. This reduces its malleability.

Hollowware An item such as a jug, bowl or teapot; as opposed to flatware.

Keying To key a surface means to scratch it mechanically with an abrasive or a file. Keying needs to be done when you are gluing parts together. A surface also needs to be keyed before painting.

Knuckles Small pieces of tube or chenier which when joined alternatively to a base and a lid, then have a pin passed through them and so become a hinge.

Lead cake A block of lead in which metal shapes can be stamped into. As the lead is soft, it allows the metal to move but supports it at the same time.

Lemel Filings and offcuts of precious metal. Worth saving for a Christmas bonus!

Malleability This is the ability of a metal to allow its shape to be changed while retaining its integrity, that is, without cracking or breaking.

Metal fatigue When metal is overworked, it loses malleability and can crack or break.

Micron 1 micron = 1/1000mm.

Milliput A two-part epoxy putty used for repairs and reforming missing pieces in (for example) sculptures. The cured putty can be painted and recoloured.

Pallion A very small piece of solder, which is the best way to control the amount of solder introduced to a joint. Stick feeding is the alternative. It is easy to add too much solder, thereby creating lots of work to remove the excess after cooling.

Patination This is the art of making a repair blend in with the original old item. This could be either darkening areas chemically that would be hard to polish, or by dulling an area that has become highly polished after repair.

Pickle A solution, used hot to clean metal after soldering and annealing. It removes oxides and flux residue. Commercial workshops use sulphuric acid in lead-lined tanks, but modern 'safety pickles' work perfectly well for the home workshop.

Piercing To saw with extremely fine blades – this technique gave rise to the term 'pierced', used when describing ornate decorative objects displaying lots of holes.

Planishing To use a flat-faced hammer to smooth dents and previous working marks. If a piece is planished correctly, very little work is required to attain a polished finish.

Reamer Larger version of a broach.

Rubbed An expression to say over-polished or worn. Engraving or hallmarks can be 'rubbed' so as to become illegible. I never polish the hallmark on a piece of silver.

Scriber Metal point for marking metal.

Split pin Split pins which are made of iron or steel can be used to hold two flat pieces together when soldering.

Sprue The channel the molten metal flows down when casting.

Stitch By using a 'V'-shaped engraver, a small tab can be raised in the surface of metal to hold another piece in position when soldering.

Swarf Metal chips or curly, sharp shards made when drilling or cutting metal.

Health and safety

There are many books written on health and safety, so I will restrict this to things particularly relevant to silversmithing to take on board. From the moment that you step into your working environment you need to be aware of any pitfalls and dangers that may lie ahead. Think about what you are doing, think what could go wrong, risk assess your activity and work in a safe manner. Do not work when you are tired or distracted. Not only could you hurt yourself but you could mess up a really precious object.

SILVERSMITH'S SECRET
Use common sense. Be careful. Be safe.

FIRE

When silversmithing, heat is invariably required. Risk assessment should be made as to the fire safety of the working area and the type of flame/heat that is going to be adopted. An escape route needs to be worked out in the event of fire. Inflammable materials should not be kept anywhere near heat or where sparks are being made. Ideally a closed metal cabinet should contain these materials.

It is important that your equipment is well maintained including the hose(es) that carry gas(es). If these have any sort of cracks or wear in them, they should be replaced.

Soldering torches are probably the most common source of heat. The area where you solder or heat needs to have fire proof bricks or similar. I also keep a jug of water nearby to cool things in and in preparation to douse any small combustion that may occur.

I always stay in my workshop for thirty minutes after the last heating operation to make sure that nothing is smouldering and that everything has cooled down safely before departure.

FIRE EXTINGUISHERS

You must also furnish your work area with fire extinguishers. I have three that I keep very close by: powder, carbon dioxide (CO_2) and water. These need to be kept in date. It is important that you know how these work and which to use for which type of fire:

Powder Safe for wood, paper and textiles, flammable liquids, gaseous fires and live electrical equipment.

CO_2 Safe for flammable liquids, live electrical equipment; not for wood, paper and textiles or flammable metal fires.

Water Safe for wood, paper and textiles; not for live electrical equipment, flammable liquids or flammable metal fires.

Fire extinguishers

The contents of an extinguisher is indicated by a coloured panel: Powder is blue, CO_2 is black, and water is red.

PRODUCTS AND CHEMICALS

Safety Data Sheets (SDS) are documents required for the safe supply, handling and use of chemicals. They help ensure that those who use chemicals in the workplace use them safely and without risk of harm to users or the environment.

The SDS will contain the information necessary to allow users to carry out a risk assessment as required by the Control of Substances Hazardous to Health Regulations (COSHH). The SDS itself is not an assessment. However, it will describe the hazards, helping users assess the probability of any potential dangers arising in the workplace.

SDSs are a must if a chemical is hazardous and is being supplied for use at work. SDS are also needed if the chemical is not classified as hazardous but contains small amounts of a hazardous substance.

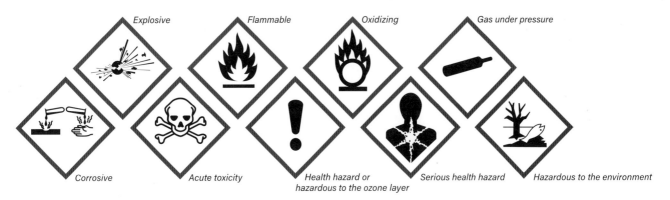

Explosive · Flammable · Oxidizing · Gas under pressure · Corrosive · Acute toxicity · Health hazard or hazardous to the ozone layer · Serious health hazard · Hazardous to the environment

First aid At a minimum in your kit should be sticky bandages, larger bandages, eye wash, alcohol and sterile tweezers.

Sharps Handle tools with sharp blades or points with care. A blunt tool that is meant to be sharp can be more dangerous to use than a sharp one.

Stakes, anvils, pitch bowls and similar tools These are all heavy. Take care not to drop them on your feet or crush your fingers when handling them.

Piercing saws Take care: I have seen people with a piercing saw blade spliced through a finger or buried behind a fingernail. It requires a trip to hospital to remove one.

Eye protection Any machine that grinds, cuts, drills or polishes can throw metal and debris into the air at high speed. Eye protection is a must when using this equipment.

Ear protection There are lots of deaf silversmiths. If you are hammering continually or grinding, wear some sort of ear protection.

Skin protection Protect your skin from any hazardous materials. I prefer nitrile gloves; they are quite thick and reusable for a while. If you are handling hot metals, then it is advisable to wear leather or heatproof gloves.

Lung protection A suitable mask should be worn if processes that give off fumes, dust or fine particles are being carried out. Chemicals should be checked and adequate PPE and ventilation should be used according to the data sheets.

Hair and loose clothing Long hair, loose clothing or jewellery can get wrapped in any rotating machine and cause injuries. Powerful bench top polishers and lathes are amongst the most dangerous machines to use. Remove loose clothing; hoodies with drawstrings are lethal. Jewellery on fingers and wrists should also be removed, and long hair tied back.

Polishing Using a bench top polishing machine can be hazardous. Familiarize yourself with the safety procedures for these machines. Most resources say that gloves should not be worn when using a rotary polisher. I sometimes do wear gloves, aware of the tiny risk. The reasons for wearing gloves are: to avoid burns (items being polished can become hot) and the polishing compounds are filthy. It is a personal choice, but users should be aware of the danger of wearing gloves.

Index